No Vision All Drive

No Vision All Drive

WHAT I LEARNED FROM MY FIRST COMPANY

Third Edition

David Brown

WILEY

Published by John Wiley & Sons, Inc., Hoboken, New Jersey.
Published simultaneously in Canada.

Edition History
AuthorHouse (1e, 2005)

For general information on our other products and services or for technical support, please contact our Customer Care Department within the United States at (800) 762-2974, outside the United States at (317) 572-3993, or fax (317) 572-4002.

Wiley publishes in a variety of print and electronic formats and by print-on-demand. Some material included with standard print versions of this book may not be included in e-books or in print-on-demand. If this book refers to media such as a CD or DVD that is not included in the version you purchased, you may download this material at http://booksupport.wiley.com. For more information about Wiley products, visit www. wiley.com.

Library of Congress Cataloging-in-Publication Data:
ISBN 978-1-119-63280-1 (hardback)
ISBN 978-1-119-63287-0 (ePDF)
ISBN 978-1-119-63285-6 (ePub)

Printed in the United States of America
V10014322_093019

Contents

Foreword, Third Edition

I t's been 15 years since I first wrote the original foreword to *No Vision All Drive,* and 26 years since David and I formed the company that would eventually become Pinpoint Technologies. In the original foreword I said that budding or experienced entrepreneurs would gain insights from David Brown's book and that people involved in rapidly scaling their company could learn a great deal from this book.

Those sentiments are still true today, but after reading this edition, I can say emphatically that people who read this book will come away with a renewed sense of purpose and actions to take that can improve their organization—regardless of whether they're involved in government, education, community building, global corporations, or entrepreneurship.

David Brown paid close attention to the people, dates, and issues involved with Pinpoint and sheds light on the ups and downs of creating a sustainable business. And although his account brings back fond memories (since I was there), he provides more than a chronological rendering of the evolution of Pinpoint. In a readable and very entertaining way, David reveals the secret sauce that made Pinpoint successful: the ethos we developed that guided our interactions with customers, employees, and potential acquirers.

I can clearly see the footprint of Pinpoint at our current company, Techstars. What we did at Pinpoint influenced Techstars' culture and guides how we treat people, how decisions are made, our commitment to knowing customers, and our relentless execution at all levels of the company. All of these are hallmarks of Techstars today, but they are the heritage of Pinpoint.

Pinpoint was not an autonomous, discrete event with a specific start and end date, but a continuous learning experience fraught with missteps, mistakes, failures . . . and success. It is the cumulation of all those experiences that have helped to form Techstars, and to David's credit, *No Vision All Drive* provides both the day-to-day effort of creating a business, along with the general principles that lead to building a sustainable business.

A realistic understanding of entrepreneurship is missing in most books on entrepreneurship, and *No Vision All Drive* fills the gap in ways that will help people with ideas get those ideas into a form that generates action and gets results.

David G. Cohen
October 2019
Boulder, Colorado

Foreword, First and Second Editions

You hold in your hands the story of the blood, sweat, and tears of hundreds of amazing people. Between 1993 and 2003, these people transformed Pinpoint Technologies from a flat-broke, shot-in-the-dark concept into a market-leading small business. This business has had a positive effect on the emergency medical services industry and has positively impacted 50 million patients in four countries.

When David Brown started writing the original version of this book in 2002, he began with a simple chronological list of the events that transpired as Pinpoint Technologies evolved over a period of 10 years. This list surprised me and made me realize just how much I was already starting to forget. It reminded me of people who were beginning to fade from memory, names that were no longer on the tip of my tongue, and events that I had recalled out of order. I immediately wanted to support the project to help solidify those precious memories. As with so many other commitments David Brown had made over the years, when he told me that he was going to take on this huge project, I knew it was going to be done and done well.

David Brown does a fantastic job in this book of capturing the very spirit of the company. What glued us all together was our commitment to a balance between having fun and creating fantastic products. A typical example was getting together for a night at the local bar and talking about how to solve a problem a customer was having. Our motto was "work hard, play hard," and it's impossible to read the book and not come away with that sense.

You will quickly realize that this is more than just another business book. David Brown outlines the reasons we were successful using interesting examples that will provide insight to any budding or experienced entrepreneur. He describes our culture, which evolved naturally and was such a key ingredient in our success. Those subscribing to the conventional wisdom found in today's rapidly growing companies can learn a great deal from this book.

It's not often that the story of a decade of your professional life is captured in writing. Memories fade with the years, but the pages of this book will always remind me of some of the best years of my life. Long after we are gone it will also tell our children and their children a little bit about who we were and what we stood for. For this and many other reasons, I am forever grateful to David Brown.

David G. Cohen
August 2004
Boulder, Colorado

Introduction

In 2004, just after leaving Pinpoint Technologies and four years after selling the company to ZOLL, I wrote the first edition of this book. My purpose then was to preserve the memories of something that David Cohen and I had built together, with help from Bob Durkin and so many others. As memories of people and events faded I wanted to preserve the story: for myself, for my family, and for anyone else who was interested. I had no idea that I would return to ZOLL for seven more years.

In 2014 my assistant at Techstars discovered the original edition and ordered a bunch of copies, and I felt compelled to read it again, probably for the first time in a decade. I had no idea that I would be gripped by it. I ended up reading it in one sitting, captured both by the trip down memory lane and by the realization of how much I have learned since I wrote the book. This third edition captures more of what I have learned about starting and scaling up, creating a culture, and managing people in a globally dispersed company.

One of the important things I learned is that words matter. A lot. This point was driven home each time I spoke with

1

someone about the book. The most frequent question I got asked was "What do you mean by 'no vision?' Isn't vision important in building a business?" At the time, in 2004, the title reflected the immense effort it took to build Pinpoint Technologies and the subtitle, "Memoirs of an Entrepreneur," seemed appropriate. But now, having been a CEO or co-CEO for the past decade, I believe that vision is one of the foundational cornerstones of building a business, and the updated version (and subtitle) of the book reflects how my thinking has changed.

When I started writing the 2004 edition, I had no idea what I would do next. I just thought I'd take a bit of a break and figure it out. Bit by bit, though, as I spent time with David, I realized that I wanted to do another startup. David, Bob, and I created iContact, which David refers to as our "graceful failure." David calls it graceful because we were able to give back our investors most of their money, but I think that it was graceful in another way, too. In creating iContact, we purposely set out to do something that we knew nothing about (mobile social networking, a B2C application that was probably as far from our core competency as possible). Its failure—and reliving the Pinpoint story when I wrote the first edition of this book—led us to realize that many of the mistakes we made were avoidable, since others had experienced them many times. This led to the notion that startups needed a better way of receiving mentorship and funding, which resulted in David and me, along with Brad Feld and Jared Polis, creating Techstars.

As I reread the first edition of this book, I couldn't help but notice how many times we were faced with huge obstacles—just like all the great startups and entrepreneurs we've worked with at Techstars. Rather than let them get the better of us, though, we plowed through them somehow and "just figured it out." I found it interesting the number times I used the words "We got lucky, because . . ." But that's what entrepreneurs do: they just figure it out.

David Brown
October 2019
Boulder, Colorado

Prelude

October 15, 1999, was in many ways the best day of my life, yet I was seething mad. We had just sold Pinpoint Technologies, a company we had built ourselves, for more money than we ever thought possible. David Cohen, Bob Durkin, and I were out to dinner with our wives at the Red Lion restaurant in the foothills above Boulder. The final days leading up to the sale had been spent frantically pulling documents from files and sending them to lawyers, staying up until the wee hours of the morning reading draft contract language, and having endless conversations about all of it with our attorney.

October 15 was the date that had been set many months earlier to close the transaction. After going to our office at 6 a.m. to finish some last-minute faxing, David, Bob, and I went to our attorney's office to sign the documents, a process that we thought would be pretty routine. We emerged 10 hours later, after having had several arguments with the other side about what felt like trivial, last-minute issues, such as the prospect of their viewing our home mortgage paperwork to confirm that we hadn't pledged the company to a bank.

In the end, the deal got done and we went out to celebrate. At the time I was furious at the attorney for the acquiring company, ZOLL, who I felt was bringing up new, unimportant issues at the eleventh hour. In hindsight, I blame our attorney for getting me worked up about these issues. It was just such a shame that such an important and exciting event caused so much frustration.

By the end of the dinner and after a few drinks, my anger had subsided and we managed to have a great time, giddy in our celebrations. We even played credit card roulette for the expensive meal, each one of us putting a credit card into a pile and letting the waiter choose. I lost.

The Birth of a Company

Pinpoint was the brainchild of David Cohen, with whom I worked at Automated Dispatch Services (ADS) in Miami. On December 7, 1993, David suggested that we start our own company. At the time we only had a vague idea of what we might do for a business, but we nevertheless went online—the Internet was virtually unheard of in 1993, but David had a CompuServe account—and created a company. Somehow I was named president and David vice president, but we both maintained the VP title for years until we became sure of our respective roles. We then talked to Bob Durkin, who had also worked with us at ADS, about our ideas and formally brought him onboard as a cofounder in 1995.

We formulated our business plan and launched our first product, RightCAD, in 1995. RightCAD was a computer-aided dispatch product for ambulance companies based in concept on a system that David and I had helped develop for ADS called EMTrack.

We had no idea early on whether we would be successful. I remember a conversation in which David and I predicted that the business would never have more than 10 employees. By the time we sold to ZOLL in 1999 there were 50 employees, and by the time I left in 2003 there were over 100. Today the company has over 250 people and it continues to be a very profitable part of ZOLL's business.

Within a decade of incorporating, Pinpoint would have $13 million a year in sales and be recognized as a leader in its industry. Yet it had been formed on a whim without a business plan by a couple of guys in their twenties who had a lot more spirit than experience. That spirit carried us through the years, allowing us to adapt to the changing environment of a growing company and to overcome the many obstacles therein. In 10 years of working together, David, Bob, and I never fought, never were petty, and never allowed egos to get in the way; in fact, we never really had any major disagreement of any kind and remain best friends. Along the way, I got to work with a lot of great people in a great environment. I can honestly say that almost every day of those 10 years was a lot of fun.

This book is an attempt to put to paper the spirit and environment that allowed us to be successful, while at the same time recounting some of the many funny and interesting experiences that happened along the way. Perhaps it will provide some insight into the things that worked well for us; perhaps it will merely be an interesting story. Regardless, I hope you enjoy it.

Chapter 1 Learning to Be an Entrepreneur

It is a mystery to me why I was drawn to the business world. My father was a longtime engineer and administrator for the city of Montreal and my mother a part-time social worker working at a children's agency. Both my parents were extremely liberal, socially conscious activists. My brother became a university professor and my sister is a health researcher, so I am the black sheep of the family. Although I consider myself a liberal and certainly lean far left on the American political spectrum, I always joke that my family considers me to be the Republican in the family.

I had what I consider to be a normal childhood full of friends and sports. I was smart and did well in school, but was never an overachiever. Once I left high school and started CEGEP (Quebec's equivalent of junior college), my priorities became friends and skiing, in that order, with academics relegated to whatever time was left. I did just enough work and attended just enough classes to get by. A career in business never occurred to me, as I thought I was more likely to become a professional hockey player or full-time ski instructor than anything else.

At CEGEP I had thoughts of being an engineer, perhaps because my father was one, but I was turned down by McGill's engineering school, the school that all my friends were going to go to. My second choice at McGill was physics, although I have no idea why. I think I might have been sitting in a physics class at CEGEP when I was filling out the form. At McGill, I quickly dropped that major when I failed my first physics class. I had done very well in a COBOL computer science class at CEGEP, programming on punch cards the year before they were completely phased out. I also had fooled around with a RadioShack CoCo computer at home, so comp sci seemed interesting, although at the time McGill only offered it in conjunction with a math degree.

Although I graduated from McGill, I never really felt I got anything out of higher education and for a time wondered why I wasted my time. Later in my career, once while in Montreal in 1988 and once while in Miami in 1991, I regretted not getting an MBA and tried to get one. I was heavily involved, if only as a witness, in the process of starting up a company, and I felt that there was a lot that I still had to learn. Twice, when my workload was low, I enrolled in an MBA program, but both times I lasted less than one semester. Eventually, work got busy again and the allure of solving problems in real life outweighed my desire for the degree.

I remain convinced, though, that an MBA would have been a good idea. Years later, at ZOLL, I got the chance to work with a number of Harvard MBAs who proved to me that there was in fact some basic knowledge that could be a great foundation for personal experience.

The Quebec Department of Transportation

My path to becoming an entrepreneur started in an unusual way: I got a job working for the government. I was a first-year student of math and computer science at McGill University in Montreal, Canada. Each year, like most students in Quebec, I filled out an application to land a provincially funded summer job. Very few students were selected each year, but as luck would have it, in 1984 my name was drawn and I got a job working for the transportation department in the software division. Back in the mid-80s, they were doing relatively cutting-edge work using mapping software to simulate traffic patterns.

The job itself was unremarkable, other than it was where I met Martin Nathanson, my direct supervisor. After working for Martin for some time, he confided in me that he was starting his own company, TransControl Systems. TransControl was creating a computer-aided dispatch software system for the courier industry. Martin offered me a job and I became employee #1.

TransControl

The computer-aided dispatch system TransControl developed was called CUSTOM 2000. Martin had signed up a Montreal-based courier company called Dicom to be TransControl's beta test site, but the business didn't progress much beyond this first customer. Although we attended some trade shows, tried to install the system at Dicom's Toronto office, and sold and installed a system in Amsterdam, TransControl was never able to develop a business model and get things off the ground.

Although CUSTOM 2000 never gained acceptance, it was far ahead of its time. Many of the features we created, such as turn-by-turn directions through a road network, are features that are still considered cutting-edge in dispatch systems today.

Martin had come up with the name CUSTOM 2000, which stood for the ridiculous "Commercial Urban Simulator for Transport Optimization and Management." When Diane Stewart joined TransControl as marketing director, she laughed at the name. Her comment was that it should stand for "a Couple of Useless Systems Technicians Orchestrated This Mess."

While at TransControl I was a programmer, but I really got to observe the pitfalls involved in being a startup company. We got some things right, but mostly I felt like the experience was a lesson in what not to do. Unfortunately, Martin was a technologist enamored with the technology and not a very good businessman.

In 1987, TransControl hooked up with John Shermyen, who was starting a company called Digital Wireless (DWC), later to be called Automated Dispatch Services (ADS) and now known as LogistiCare.

John and his partner Jim Smith were trying to start a company that would buy up and consolidate other ambulance companies. This idea was also ahead of its time and would catch on five or so years later, when companies like AMR, Rural/Metro, and MedTrans would very successfully launch a consolidation trend. John was interested in TransControl because he wanted to adapt the computer-aided dispatch system we had created for couriers to ambulances.

Initially, TransControl and DWC had a joint-venture arrangement. Eventually, in November of 1989, John got $1 million in funding from venture capitalists and bought out

Martin's share for $70,000. The $1 million was to fund the creation of a dispatch center in Miami. Around that time, I had become quite disillusioned with TransControl. The work we had done was not yielding customers and although we had grown to a dozen employees, finances were very tight and interest in our product was minimal.

> As part of the funding deal, DWC changed its name to Automated Dispatch Services (ADS), which was a better reflection of their business.

> In a story typical of TransControl, we had one customer in Montreal and another in Toronto when, somehow, we managed to sell a system in Amsterdam. With only two local customers under our belt, we became convinced that this was a great international product and started attending trade shows in London. We went to an enormous amount of work to have our GIS guy, Tommy Marinos (who was self-taught and straight out of school), digitize the complex London street network by hand, which was an impossible task. This and many other similar experiences at both TransControl and ADS taught me one of the most important lessons in business: the importance of focus.

DWC/ADS

In December 1989, John Shermyen flew me down to Miami, where he had landed a contract with Medicar Ambulance to do all of their dispatching. While it wasn't the consolidation concept that he had originally conceived of, it was still a pretty novel idea, as Medicar would pay ADS on a pay-per-run basis to staff a call center to answer calls and dispatch ambulances. It is still a mystery to me why an ambulance company would want to outsource one of the most important components of their business, but the deal was a testament to John's incredible sales ability.

At the core of the Miami center was EMTrack, the computer-aided dispatch software that had been adapted from the courier system created by TransControl. Adapting the courier version of EMTrack was challenging, and there were a lot of issues that made the product difficult to use in the ambulance environment. EMTrack never really worked well until it was completely rewritten in a project we called Rev II.

I enjoyed Miami. Each year, thousands of snowbirds from Canada descend on the Florida beaches in an effort to escape the brutally cold Montreal winters. While the idea of the beautiful weather had always appealed to me, I had this image of Florida as a place with neon-lit palm trees and tacky tourist shops littered all over the place. I was wrong about that. Florida is a state with beautiful landscapes, parks, beaches, friendly people, great food, and a deep history. John did a great job of welcoming me, finding an apartment for me on Miami Beach, and taking me out on the town.

In a crazy side story very typical of my time in Miami, my apartment belonged to the father of the owner of Medicar, who used it as a getaway to shack up with young Russian women he helped to immigrate into the US. I never knew for sure, but rumor had it that they spent time as prostitutes in exchange for this help.

I thought I was in Miami to help resolve some software issues. Never in a million years did I think they were going to make me a job offer. Jim Smith was the one who did it. I think he couldn't stand how long John took to get to the point. As soon as he saw me, Jim said, "So, do you want to come down here to work full time?"

I had never even considered leaving Montreal. It was the city in which I was born and raised, and I expected to live my life and die there. Yet, John and Jim's timing couldn't have been better. Most of my friends had left town after college and my longtime girlfriend and I had just split, so staying in Montreal had lost a lot of its appeal. I quickly made up my mind and accepted the job on the spot. I went back to Montreal for three days, packed up, and got back on a plane to Miami to start work. I was 25 years old and completely enamored with the risk-taking John Shermyen; his enthusiasm was completely contagious to me.

> The story of moving to the United States was actually pretty funny, at least in hindsight. After packing all of my belongings into my car, I went to a friend's wedding. During the wedding, my car was stolen along with all of the stuff in it. So I bought a pair of jeans and a few T-shirts and jumped on a plane without a possession in the world. Talk about a fresh start!

A rational person might have worried about how he was going to get a work permit to work in the United States, how ADS would be funded, and whether the product or service model John was proposing would even be feasible, but I didn't worry about any of those things. I just thought, "I love the US because people there are willing to bet the farm every day to chase their dreams." I accepted the job at $36,000 a year.

The work permit story would of course become much more complicated. At the time I accepted the job, John said, "Don't worry, I've done this many times before," referring to the fact that Jim had run the Mariel boat lift operation for the US government, when Castro opened his jails and thousands of Cubans poured into South Florida. I still have no idea if this story is true, but Jim's experience certainly didn't help me a bit with the Immigration and Naturalization Service. I came down on a renewable one-year work permit, and eventually, after two years of waiting for John, had to retain an immigration attorney myself to get a green card.

Gainesville

While I liked Miami, I didn't really want to live in Florida. John was putting the finishing touches on a deal that would create a California dispatch center similar to the one in Miami, and my plan was to move to Long Beach as soon as it opened.

It was a typical John Shermyen sales job: he never actually told me that the deal in California was as good as done, but I wanted it to happen badly enough that I inferred it was. Later, around the time David Cohen came onboard with ADS, we were working on a deal to open an office in Atlanta, and David was made a similar promise, only to see it fall through. As crazy as it sounds, this happened a third time—with a deal we were working in Denver—with Bob, who had always wanted to move to Colorado. David, Bob, and I still firmly believe that California, Atlanta, and Denver were real deals and that we never felt lied to. However, none of these three centers ever got off the ground.

While waiting for the California deal to get done, I temporarily moved to ADS headquarters in Gainesville, in central Florida, to help create Rev II, the next version of EMTrack. I was teaching skiing in Canada on the weekends at the time, and my friends, the ski instructors, could not understand my desire to move to Florida, a state with no snow. California made even less sense to them.

Another great anecdote that should have tipped me off about things to come was that when I got off the plane for my first day with ADS, John greeted me at the airport, but had to borrow money to get his car out of the parking lot. We then went by the bank so he could get a cash advance on his personal credit card to make payroll. Strangely, this didn't worry me.

Gainesville was a strange place for me to live, especially for my first experience of living in the US. In addition to having to get used to the differences between the US and Canada—such as how litigious everyone was and how lawyers advertised on TV—I had to get used to living in what I considered to be a small college town. I adjusted to life in Gainesville by traveling a lot. Of the nine months I lived in Gainesville, six were spent on the road traveling to various places around the US.

Before my arrival, John had hired Andy Winner to support the code that John had purchased from TransControl. Andy, as many programmers would, felt the product would be better if it were rewritten from scratch. By the time I arrived, work had already begun on what Andy and John were calling Rev II, a rewritten version of EMTrack. I supported this idea and saw my role as patching Rev I wherever possible in order to keep it going until Rev II was ready. At the same time, I filled a role I now know as product management, feeding Andy information about what customers and users wanted so that he could implement it in Rev II.

Rev II was developed using C and stored its data in a Novell-based database called Btrieve. For 1990, the technology Andy had selected was cutting-edge. Btrieve was a client-server architecture and abstracted a lot of the functions into the database itself. In addition, it came with a rudimentary yet flexible report-writing package called Xtrieve.

Eventually, we rolled out Rev II into the Miami center. The product was so buggy that ambulance dispatchers wanting to update the status of one trip had to position the cursor on the trip above it. That they were willing to put up with this goes to show how bad Rev I really was.

Ultimately, John sold EMTrack to a number of ambulance companies, but none found the product to be very functional. I spent most of my time traveling around to these customers, patching up the product to try to get it to work. One of the problems was John's habit of selling vaporware (software features that didn't exist yet). This was an important experience for me and a huge example of what not to do, which David, Bob, and I carried through to our Pinpoint days.

There were ultimately a total of 12 EMTrack sites, with 6 of those handed to us by a company called Ambpac, a developer of billing software for ambulance companies.

Eventually, the California center idea fell through, and I was faced with the prospect of moving to the Miami center or staying in Gainesville. I decided to move to Miami.

In fact, there was no actual "move" to Miami. I was there on a business trip and decided to stay. John, who lived in Gainesville, loaded all my belongings into the back of his pickup truck and drove them down to Miami for me.

Miami

I relocated to Miami in the fall of 1990 and lived for a couple of months with Tommy Marinos, who had also been hired away from TransControl, before I bought a place of my own in Coconut Grove. I worked very hard and didn't have much of a social life. While I hung out a bit with fellow ADS employees Efrain Cuellar and his sister Maria, I spent most of my time keeping the software at the Miami center running and traveling the country, trying to keep EMTrack customers happy.

Efrain did general technical support of the EMTrack product and Maria was in charge of the Miami center. Both were bright and dedicated to ADS and John Shermyen, although we used to joke that if Maria didn't get to fire a person a week, she would be in a bad mood. Although Maria and I would eventually be at odds and would have a hard time getting along, initially we were great friends and would go out socially.

STS

In June of 1991, the Miami center got a contract to dispatch the Special Transportation Service, known as STS. Even before the Americans with Disabilities Act made it law to provide programs for people with disabilities, Dade County had a very progressive program whereby all people with disabilities could get door-to-door transportation to wherever they wanted to go for a $2 co-pay. The program had been in place for many years and about 1,500 people took advantage of it an average of twice a day. The contract to move these people from A to B (or back to A) each day was with a company called Metro Limo, one of Miami's larger taxi companies.

Metro Limo was run by three shady characters named Ziggy, Eddie, and Marty. Eddie Steinberg was the very overweight, profane, sweaty guy who ran the day-to-day operations. John somehow convinced the trio to outsource the entire call-taking and dispatch operation to ADS.

> I can remember sitting in a meeting with Eddie and a bunch of his cronies in which John and I were basically explaining why something we had done had gone wrong. I made the mistake of saying that I had assumed something and then had to listen to Eddie, with sweat dripping off his chin onto the conference table, explain for many minutes how when you "assume" you make an "ass" out of "u" and "me."

I learned a great deal when we took over the STS operation. I'm not sure that John had thought through how complex the logistics were of taking over such a large operation. Not only did 50 people or so have to leave Metro Limo and start working for ADS in a different location, but there were phone issues, computer issues, and all kinds of other things to be taken care of.

I used to describe the process of making sure that 3,000 people got from A to B as being like balancing a pyramid upside down. It's hard to get just right, and if you do get it right, all it takes is a small wind to knock it over. In the same way, the process of setting up the next day started around 4 p.m. and went all night. If you got behind and didn't get the routes printed out for the drivers, morning riders would be picked up late and the whole schedule would be thrown off, causing phone calls from people wanting to know where their ride was. The delays would then snowball because the extra phone calls took up our time and therefore caused even more people to be late.

I remember that the first two days after we took over STS were so hectic that I only got two hours of sleep each night. Within a week, Maria and I were so exhausted that we went to John and were willing to throw in the towel. We actually looked into it, but it would have taken a couple of weeks for the phone company to switch the lines back, and by then things were a little more under control.

Bit by bit, we learned how to run a transportation company, both from a management and a technical standpoint. One of the things that gave ADS an advantage was our computer capability, which we used to the greatest extent possible. Once the basics of the dispatch system were up and running, I viewed a big part of my job as sitting in the center, learning everyone's job, and figuring out how we could make it easier through automation. Anytime someone used a pen I'd try to figure out how to prevent it from happening again.

EMTrack became a strong dispatch product because of its proximity to a high-volume user. The continuous improvement cycle was so rapid that things became increasingly efficient. This was an important lesson that I would later take to Pinpoint.

The Orlando Center

In September of 1991, with the Miami center barely under control, ADS somehow got a contract to answer calls and dispatch drivers for a Medicaid program in Orlando. For $2.58 per call, ADS was to provide software, call takers, and dispatchers, basically everything that was needed other than the vehicles and the drivers. It would be a fateful contract, not because of its impact on ADS (it was a small center), but because that is where I would meet David Cohen and Bob Durkin, my future Pinpoint cofounders.

I traveled up to the Orlando center as it was preparing to go live. The ADS contract was with a government entity called the Regional Planning Council. The RPC had assigned one of their IT people, David Cohen, to help with the project.

John and I could both sense that David was more one of us than one of them. I worked late into the night with David, teaching him everything I knew about EMTrack. The RPC employees were all out the door at 5 p.m., but David, John, and I were in do-what-you-have-to-do-to-get-this-thing-working mode.

I vividly remember how impressed I was with David's technical ability. By this time, I had trained a lot of people on EMTrack, but I'd never found anyone who understood issues and remembered details like David did. It was like we were one and the same: I told him once, he absorbed, and we moved on. Very quickly, we were equals.

After about a week in the Orlando center, I left to return to Miami. Meanwhile, things at the Orlando center were a disaster operationally. There weren't enough dispatchers, call takers, or managers, all of which contributed to all of our trips being late. The software was live, yet we didn't have the staff or the office setup to run it.

When desks arrived unassembled, David suggested that his college roommate, Bob Durkin, might be interested in assembling the desks for some extra cash, which ended up being only $20 a desk. John quickly realized that Bob was bright and hired him to take calls, then promoted him to dispatcher, and later to manager of the entire center.

The Syracuse Center

Shortly after Orlando opened, John started another center, in Syracuse, New York. This one was relatively simple, because it was already an existing EMTrack customer, Eastern Ambulance (now Rural/Metro). We took over the operation, started paying the same employees who used to work for Eastern, and charged Eastern a fee for each call we ran.

It turned out the reason John got the contract with Eastern was that they were frustrated with EMTrack. In an effort to placate them, John had convinced them that the users weren't using the system properly.

"Let them work for me," John said, "and I'll make sure they get properly trained."

Of course, the problem was with EMTrack, so training didn't help. John made the dispatch manager for Eastern, Ed Moser, our center manager for Syracuse, and then we promptly ignored them.

After a while Eastern realized that this arrangement wasn't working, so they kicked us out and purchased another software package from American TriTech, our big competitor in the early Pinpoint days.

The Miami Center

In late 1991, as the Orlando center ramped up, it required more attention. John brought up the manager of the Miami center, Maria Cuellar, to Orlando to help out.

That vacancy allowed me to take on a management role running the Miami center. While I had spent quite a bit of time there, it was in an IT support role, helping with problems with the EMTrack product or getting a better understanding of user requirements to be implemented into the product.

Suddenly I was in charge of 50 or so call takers and dispatchers. There was a massive difference between these line-level workers and the professionals I had worked with previously. Overall, they were a great bunch of people, but they were from a world unknown to me. There were a lot of 20-year-old single mothers, living with their parents, making $5 an hour. Their stories were sad and difficult, but hearing about the events happening around them was a part of my job and they took on a comical nature. Life was bizarre, but it seemed normal to us at the time. There were countless stories of lunches being stolen, employees (female) beating each over the head with radios, relatives being murdered or arrested, and parole officer visits. It wasn't until this time that I realized that I had grown up in a life of privilege. The experience was a real eye-opener for me.

As part of my new job as center manager I now had to attend customer feedback sessions, called C-SAIL, that were held once a month on Sunday mornings. Invariably it was a bitch session, where we sat on a panel with representatives of the transportation company and the county while countless people wanted to know why their ride was late on a certain day, why a driver was rude to them, or why we had taken them in this direction instead of that one. These sessions were completely unproductive and I dreaded them. With so many transports being done, it was impossible to have on-the-spot answers for even legitimate questions. The whole Sunday morning experience had a feeling of get in and out as quickly as possible.

A better memory from the C-SAIL meetings was getting to know some of the riders, including a blind couple, Otto and Leah, who met through their activism in reforming our service. Because we booked their transportation, we had some insight into their lives, and I remember our call taker Sandra being very excited the first time Otto booked an overnight trip to stay at Leah's apartment. Sandra and I, along with a number of other ADS employees, subsequently were invited to their wedding.

David Cohen

Born in DeLand, Florida, near Orlando, David had been a Florida boy all his life. He went to school at University of

Central Florida in Orlando, where his roommates were Bob Durkin and Devon McClain, another longtime Pinpoint employee and David's future brother-in-law. After college, he had gotten a job with the RPC for $19,000 a year.

> David has always been a famously quick learner. When he found out that the job at the RPC required knowledge of Paradox, he immediately added it to his resume, even though he had no experience with it. He then read up on it in time to know enough to get him through the interview. When he got the job, he made sure he completely understood the program before he started work. Then, as he tells it, it was never required in his duties. I've always told that story as an example of when it might be permissible to bend the truth: it's okay as long as you deliver.

Soon after I became center manager in Miami, David Cohen accepted a position with ADS where, among other things, he wrote a billing system that took data out of EMTrack and interfaced it with the state Medicaid system.

Because the Orlando center was much smaller and we were supporting the dozen or so EMTrack sites from Miami, John asked David to relocate. David accepted, but thought it was temporary until the Atlanta center opened. Somehow, John talked me into having David as a roommate. I remember picking David up at the Miami airport in early 1992 after having only met him for the week that we worked in Orlando together.

David and I got along right away. We both jumped into problems and got them resolved. That's why John liked having us around. John quickly put David in charge of supporting the various EMTracks around the country, including in the Miami center, allowing me to focus on managing the center.

In those early days, David and I would each get paged every single night. It could be for an EMTrack issue or it could be for a staffing issue. Because of the massive number of calls being dispatched in the center, a single sick call taker or dispatcher could disrupt an entire day. Generally, when my pager or David's pager went off we would both get out of bed, waiting to hear what had happened so we could judge if the crisis was minor enough for one of us to go back to bed.

After I became center manager, Tommy Marinos became the development manager. Politically, it just didn't seem right to put David in charge of the programmers, as he had just started. Within a couple of weeks, though, it became apparent that David was much more qualified than Tommy and he took over the management role while Tommy returned to map development. David had three programmers working for him: Andy Winner, Joe Tozzi, and a strange bird named Eran Shay.

Eran

Eran was ultimately the guy who wrote 80 percent of RightCAD and Sanitas at Pinpoint. In 1991 he wrote a letter to John Shermyen saying that he couldn't get a job because of lack of experience and was willing to work for free. John hired him for $100 a week. David and I quickly realized that Eran had an unbelievable amount of raw programming talent. He was, and still is, a brute force programmer, developing features that are elegant from the user's point of view but always coded in a highly disorganized way.

A recent immigrant from Israel, Eran had a hard time adapting to the US. He lacked many basic social skills and would peer around pillars to look at cute girls. He quickly learned that credit card companies would give him credit, which he viewed as being the same as cash, which he immediately spent. Bob and I would take him out to bars where he would guzzle hard liquor and become immediately intoxicated. As hard as we tried, he never did quite fit in with the rest of the world.

From a professional standpoint, however, the product took off with Eran's help. Although the core EMTrack product was written and maintained by Andy Winner, David quickly assigned Eran to multiple useful side projects, such as a reporting program called JATREP (Job, Alpha, and Time sequence REPort), a routing program, a new way to route called the Watch screen, a program to automatically call for taxis called "cabcalls," and an end-of-night process called "the button" that would clean up data, print reports, and do backups. David even created a program that automatically faxed out a lunch order, which was straightforward since we ate the same thing every day. David and Eran also embarked on an important project to stabilize EMTrack and create an easy-to-use installation program for new EMTrack users, all experience that would become useful later on at Pinpoint.

Bob Durkin

For a long time, my exposure to Bob had only been from stories from David, John, Maria, or the odd phone call that we had. He was running Orlando and I was running Miami and sometimes he would call with questions on how we had done things.

In early 1993, the Orlando office looked like it was going to close down. Simultaneously, we were having trouble with

JC, one of the supervisors in the Miami center. John basically gave me a choice of keeping JC or having Bob come down to Miami to be the assistant manager. The choice was obvious and Bob moved down. Initially, Bob stayed on my couch in our Coconut Grove townhouse.

David Cohen, Bob Durkin, and I were now all working and living together.

> David and I had developed a tradition of waking up early on Saturday mornings and watching *Saved by the Bell* and *Degrassi Junior High* together. Once Bob moved in, this drove him crazy. Bob worked the late shift at the Miami center and we would invariably wake him up to watch what he considered to be two incredibly stupid shows. To make matters worse, after the shows were done, we could then go back to sleep, but he couldn't.

At the office, Bob always said that he was my hatchet man. In theory I worked from 6 a.m. to 2 p.m. and Bob worked from 2 p.m. to 10 p.m., although I actually worked from 6 a.m. to 6 p.m. and Bob worked from 10 a.m. to 10 p.m. When we had to let someone go, which was often, we always did it at the end of the shift, which resulted in Bob getting to do the honors. Bob always joked that nobody liked it when he asked them to come into the office.

Managing the Miami Center

The environment of managing the Miami dispatch center is best described in a series of stories.

The STS program provided affordable transportation for people with disabilities. It also allowed a single companion to travel with the passenger. One of our regulars was problematic, because she was a blind single mother with two children. Under a strict application of the rules, only one child could travel with her, since only one companion was allowed. The county administrators made a special exception in her case.

We always had enormous difficulty in processing the exceptions. There were more than 3,000 daily riders in the STS program and we prerouted all the trips the night before. Because the routers weren't accustomed to allowing room in the vehicle for two companions, her trips were often messed up.

Her complaints made their way up the chain until I eventually got a call from the office of a county commissioner asking me to make sure that her Sunday trip to church with her two children went off without a hitch.

What could I do? I personally made sure that the routers gave her one of our most reliable drivers (a man named Siddiqi) and that nobody else was scheduled to be in the vehicle at the same time. I informed our weekend manager, Elaine Taylor, about the situation and made sure that she personally contacted Siddiqi an hour before the scheduled pickup to make sure everything would proceed smoothly.

At the scheduled time, Siddiqi, a devout Muslim, arrived at the house and knocked on her door. When she answered, she was completely nude. He turned around and left without her.

One day, I was having a conversation with my friend Amy Robillard about the types of management situations I faced in the Miami center. I remember her saying, "You must deal with a lot of strange situations." So I told her two stories from the previous day: (1) A friend of one of our drivers had called in to say that the driver wouldn't be making it in to work, as he had been arrested for having drowned his wife in the bathtub. (2) A call taker called in sick, saying she was too distraught over the death of her uncle to come in to work. It turned out that the uncle was crushed in a garbage truck while attempting an escape from prison.

One of the best characters working at the center was a dispatcher named Julio Perez. Julio, who'd always wanted to be called Hector until he later changed his name to Peter Kane, was a convicted drug smuggler, and he told fantastic stories of sinking million-dollar yachts to hide evidence. But after his release from prison, he went to work for us, making $7 per hour on the graveyard shift. A couple of Drug Enforcement Agency guys sat in the parking lot all night and followed him wherever he went.

It was a regular occurrence for me to receive visits from the parole officers of our employees. Mostly they were just checking to see whether the employees had told us that they were on parole before we hired them.

One of the most important things I learned in the Miami center was the importance of understanding where people were coming from. When Bob moved down from Orlando to become the assistant manager of the Miami center, I spent the better part of a week filling him in on all the employees, what made them tick, and what they were like. I've always felt that if you understand your employees and their needs, you can provide a much better work environment for them and benefit by way of greater productivity.

A positive aspect of the Miami center was its proximity to the programmers. When I had been in charge of development, I spent most of my day in the center, working with the users. I even worked several shifts as a call taker and an ambulance dispatcher. I always called myself an EMTrack dispatcher, but unlike the professionals, I would never have been able to dispatch had it not been for the computer system.

I developed a great working relationship with David. As the center manager and a reasonably technical person, I knew best what functionality would make our staff's job easier. I fed that information to David, who would implement it. Later, we tried to replicate that environment at Pinpoint by having a product manager who was an expert on what was needed from the customer point of view and a program manager who was in charge of implementing those features. The product manager and the program manager had a peer relationship and had to work together to figure out what was best. We never achieved, however, the rapid identification of issues and the quick definition of features that was possible when the users were just across the hall.

Hurricane Andrew

On August 24, 1992, David and I were up in Orlando visiting Bob and some friends. The Saturday night news said that a Category 5 (the highest level) hurricane was heading straight for Miami.

Since the Miami center dispatched about half the ambulances in Miami, I knew that we would have to stay open as long as we could during the storm, so I hurried home. I was lucky, because just after I got back the government turned the interstate into lanes all going north, as people were trying to get away from the storm.

I went home and did the best I could to protect my house, getting everything off the floor and away from the windows in case of flooding. Following a suggestion I had seen on TV, I filled the bathtub for drinking water and headed to the office. Later on, I was so hot from lack of air conditioning and showers that I rashly took a bath in the water I had saved up for drinking.

I parked my car in the lobby of our building—yes, you read that right, the lobby. I had a Jeep Wrangler that was small enough to fit through the doors. Otherwise, I'm quite certain I would never have seen it again. I sprinted up to our office on the fourth floor and got ready for the storm.

Our building was 10 miles inland, so I thought we should be pretty safe. But it was still frightening. I could see our thick windows bend in the wind. Going down to the lobby to check on my car seemed too risky.

Obviously, we shut down all nonemergency portions of the company, which left only a skeleton crew to dispatch the ambulances. Hector took the helm as the main dispatcher as Miami Beach evacuated. We transported patients back and forth out of the hospitals to safer locations. As the crews did their last runs at about 11 p.m., I remember Hector lining them up in a four-by-four formation to protect them from the incredible winds while crossing the causeway from Miami Beach.

After that, we sort of didn't know what to do. Nobody could go outside and the ambulance crews were all placed in shelters in case of medical problems. Eventually the power went out and I tried to get a couple of hours of sleep in the center of the office, away from the windows.

In an illustration of how overworked our computer servers were, I did maintenance on them while the hurricane was over us. After the ambulances were off the road and until the power went out and the battery backup ran out, I shut down the terminals and did some much-needed archiving. Since the Miami center ran 24 hours a day, seven days a week, this was a rare opportunity to do some intensive work that couldn't be done if users were using the system. I took full advantage, but then the server crashed and the power went out, leaving me to deal with it later somehow.

When John Shermyen took people on a tour of the center, the battery backup was always a centerpiece of the tour. It was a huge machine, about the size of a refrigerator, and was supposed to power the whole center for 24 hours in the event of a power failure. Hurricane Andrew was the only time we got to put it to the test and it lasted just a couple of hours with only a couple of computers running. I eventually had to run out to a store and use some ambulance credentials to cut in front of an unbelievably long line to buy a generator.

The storm veered south at the last minute and missed Miami Beach, but hit south Miami very hard. Once the winds died down and it was safe to go outside, the ambulances started rolling again. It turned out that the storm badly damaged Kendall Hospital, where we had taken a lot of the Miami Beach patients. These poor folks had to be evacuated again!

Two days after the storm, I ventured outside to go see how my house had fared. I was nervous, as I lived less than a mile from the ocean. On the way home, I passed the airport and saw a 727 tilted on its nose. Traffic lights and electrical wires were hanging everywhere, volunteers were trying to direct traffic, and I saw a boat on the highway about a mile inland. It looked like a war zone.

Within a couple of days, after power was restored at the airport, David was able to fly back from Orlando to help out. He took the crashed server to Efrain's house, which was in one of the few areas of the city that had electricity, to get it going while I was dealing with operations. David and I were living together, and the power was still out, so we continued to sleep at the office. I remember that we would call home on a regular basis and it was a happy day when the answering machine answered, because that meant that the power was back on.

The thing I remember most about my experience is how bad the weeks after the storm were. I was lucky that I was in a safe building during the storm, but for weeks afterward there was no food to be bought in the stores, no running water, no electricity, no gas for the car, and no services whatsoever, all against the backdrop of dreadful Miami heat. Eventually the army came in and set up tent cities for those who had lost their homes. The navy sent a big ship that docked in Miami Harbor with 10,000 cooks onboard who made meals for those who needed them.

South Miami, which received the direct hit from the hurricane, was a crazy place for a long time. Looting was commonplace. Ice and suntan lotion sold on the black market for exorbitant prices. People spray-painted the sides of their condemned homes with signs such as "You loot, we shoot," or with their insurance information, so that the insurance companies could process their claims.

It was amazing to me how quickly business people started to capitalize on opportunities created by the hurricane. Before I had even absorbed the enormity of what had happened,

John, Eddie Steinberg, and the others were scrambling to get in on some of the FEMA money that was flying around. ADS got a contract to dispatch free rides being given out to those in heavily damaged south Miami, which we imaginatively called South Dade Free Ride (SDFR). The contract was run by Handi-Van, one of ADS's original customers, which was run by a very classy lady named Masi Neff. Handi-Van and ADS made an enormous amount of money on the SDFR program with almost no overhead—we dispatched the whole program with one individual named Baldo.

The worst effects of the hurricane were felt in Miami for well over a year. It took a long time to rebuild houses and get services up and running again. It was estimated that more than one third of houses in south Miami were either damaged or destroyed. When you watch news coverage of a hurricane on TV, you lack the perspective of how much damage is being done and how huge the area is. In addition, TV coverage tends to end after the storm passes, which is when the real problems are only beginning.

For David, Bob, and me, Hurricane Andrew, like STS and Orlando, was a great lesson in crisis management. In an environment that was unfamiliar, chaotic, and constantly changing, our jobs were to bring order to the chaos. It required us to be decisive, creative, and open minded. These were skills that would serve us well.

Living in Miami

In 1993, David, Bob, and I still lived in Miami. Although I always lived in the same condo, David and Bob seemed to move in and out of different homes all the time. For a while they lived in a nice home on Bayshore Drive owned by the president of Medicar. John also stayed there when he was in Miami, which was often five days a week even though he lived in Gainesville.

We were typical twentysomethings. We stayed up at night watching *Saturday Night Live*, and we had nicknames for our girlfriends (mostly Bob's) and acquaintances, like Rubber Dress Chick, Punk Rock Chick, Roller Blade Chick, Planet Moon, and Hairy Cleavage.

In one of the few unembarrassing stories I can recall, I remember waking up one morning to the sound of the dryer. This was strange to me, as our washing machine was broken.

"What are you doing?" I asked David.

"Don't you know about the formula?" he asked.

"What formula?" I said.

"Warm = Clean," said David.

While we were generally being goofballs in the off-hours, we were certainly united and driven when it came to work. John was keeping us challenged with new contracts and ideas, and David, Bob, and I had to rush out and figure out how to implement them from both a technical and management perspective. We'd often go out to dinner or sit around someone's home with John and talk about things, only to have to make them a reality in the days to come.

I cannot overemphasize how much all three of us loved to be around John. His enthusiasm was infectious, and it was great to go out to dinner with him to discuss the minutiae of what was going on. He'd even have our bookkeeper Susan's sister, a hairdresser, come into his office to cut everyone's hair while we talked to him.

It was without a doubt the most creative and free-flowing time of my life, and certainly taught the three of us how to get things done.

Selling EMTrack

ADS was in the business of selling its fee-for-service dispatch services. John liked this model because once a company signed up, they continued to pay a fee every month for life. Occasionally, we would come across an ambulance company that would be interested in buying EMTrack. We never went looking for them—we didn't attend many trade shows and we didn't advertise or have a brochure—but sometimes they would find us.

John was always happy to sell them a copy of EMTrack. He had one all-inclusive price for this—$50,000—which would buy you an unlimited number of users, all the features, and lifetime support. ADS always seemed to be living on the edge financially, so John was very happy to get the cash.

John Shermyen was a dreamer and a visionary. He envisioned everything that was not and paid little attention to everything that was. Luckily for ADS, John Shermyen could sell anything to anyone, even if it didn't exist. Before the word "vaporware" was popular, ADS had mastered it. We explored everything from riverboat captaining to cellular long-distance plans based outside the country. John would convince the prospect and the entire company that his latest idea was not far off from the capabilities that we had and that the EMTrack software could easily be molded into what would be required. Soon, we all found ourselves actually believing it. This was a vicious cycle, because when we had to actually deliver, we would.

Because David, Bob, and I were responsible for the implementation of the vaporware that John sold, avoiding those situations became ingrained in us in the Pinpoint days. Our standard story was that John always talked about how EMTrack interfaced to any phone system. Not only is every phone system different, making such a generic interface impossible, but EMTrack didn't even interface to the ADS phone system! In the Pinpoint days, we considered it a firing offense to sell something we didn't have.

Another lesson we learned in the ADS days was to avoid selling hardware. EMTrack was sold as a total solution, complete with computers, server, and wiring. After countless installs in which we were pulling cable and supporting broken keyboards, we finally experimented with selling only the software. We found that customers could purchase their hardware from Dell or a local computer vendor, who would provide support and an experience that was just as good. Meanwhile, our experience would be infinitely better.

John had sold a number of copies of EMTrack through Ambpac, a billing software company. Ambpac had presold a number of dispatch systems to their customers but had difficulty implementing the systems, so they bought EMTrack for these customers to fulfill their obligation. Because customers had bought from a different company, there was never a clear understanding as to whether EMTrack met their needs, so the customers, ADS, and Duncan Waldrip, the president of Ambpac, were often at odds. This relationship between Ambpac and ADS would come back to haunt us in the Pinpoint days.

Initially I was only involved in the installation and support aspects of these systems. It wasn't until an ambulance company named TWC purchased EMTrack in 1991 that I was involved in the sales process. TWC was an ambulance company in Long Island, New York, owned by a guy named Al Liguori. Al came to an American Ambulance Association trade show in Nashville in late 1990 specifically looking for a dispatch system. ADS was exhibiting EMTrack and Al became very interested in it.

As part of the decision-making process, Al wanted his dispatch manager to participate in the system selection so that there would be buy-in from the end users of the system. That dispatch manager, John Stapleton, would ultimately become one of the early Pinpoint employees.

The experience with TWC was the first time that I realized that EMTrack could be sold using a cookie-cutter approach. Al had a no-nonsense approach; he simply wanted to know what the software could do and wanted to run his operation around that. It was the reverse of what I had been used to, with potential customers demanding features and ADS promising vaporware.

After TWC, we encountered other companies, like Midwood, Five Counties, and NationWide, which were selling software-only systems with no vaporware. It was an epiphany for David and me; selling software could be easy.

Over the years ADS sold around a dozen EMTrack systems, primarily in the New York area. David and I did the implementation and support of these systems, so we learned how to fine-tune our approach. By 1994, just before I left ADS, I had sold my first EMTrack system on my own and had therefore overseen the complete process: from sale to deployment to support.

SkyWire and Vendview

A fluke relationship between John Shermyen and a company called SkyWire would set in motion some ideas that would ultimately lead to David and my creating a Microsoft Windows–based dispatch product and starting Pinpoint.

John had somehow met a silver-spoon-fed fellow, named Brian, who was toying with a new company called SkyWire. SkyWire's concept was to wirelessly enable vending machines. The vending machine would signal low-quantity conditions, break-in attempts, and unscheduled door openings. SkyWire would monitor coin and product levels, sending periodic updates to a central location. All of this would help the vendor to keep his costs low and give him the ability to monitor his kingdom from afar.

Naturally, John Shermyen saw a perfect fit for ADS. Part of what we did was dispatch, and vending machines have people dispatched to them. He convinced SkyWire of the virtues of a map-based system that would show alarms and allow you to zoom in on vending machines. The fact that EMTrack did neither of these things very well in relation to the vending machine industry was an overlooked detail. To John, this was interesting, and interesting mattered more than anything.

John and David met with Brian when SkyWire was a two-man company operating out of a private home. Brian had somehow convinced Coca-Cola that this was a viable project and they had agreed to work toward a pilot test for the project. John negotiated a 25-cent per vending machine per month royalty with SkyWire, and a deal was struck.

But repurposing our ambulance software and creating a wireless vending machine monitoring application was not enough of a challenge for John. He had also promised to create the application to run on Microsoft Windows. This was new technology and not yet popular. But SkyWire insisted, so John agreed. Not only would we have to learn a new industry, we would have to rewrite all the EMTrack code that could be used for a new platform that none of us had ever seen before.

At the time, Windows programming was new. No one on staff at ADS had ever done it, so David set out to learn about it. He bought Borland C++ version 1.0 and began to experiment. Tommy Marinos began to try to develop some mapping technology for both EMTrack and the VendView application. He located a third-party outfit called Etak that could supply Windows-compatible code and map data. Tommy was able to integrate the Etak mapping system into the vending machine tracking application and David wrote much of the database management system. What we ended up with was a fairly rudimentary but interesting prototype that we called VendView.

David traveled to Memphis, taking with him the latest version of VendView so that SkyWire could critique it. While there he took notes and we implemented the desired changes when he returned to Miami. This cycle continued for about six months, until SkyWire felt it was a good enough prototype. A company in New York, Ademco, made the spread-spectrum radios that the Coke machines were to be equipped with. From Miami, we were able to use modems to dial into a Coke machine in New York and another in Memphis. This was our only source of real-time data to test the application with. It was neat to be able to see how much money and soda were in the machines hundreds of miles away.

During this time, Eran, Tommy, and David became familiar with the basics of Windows software. Around the office and at home, David would often discuss his findings with me. I even tried my hand at using C++ after one long discussion about the future of object-oriented programming. After many late nights, we decided that Windows was the future.

Chapter 2 The Idea for Pinpoint Technologies

Somehow David and I got in the habit of having dinner every Wednesday night in a ritual that we called PHK. We'd leave work early, around 5 p.m., go to Pizza Hut for dinner, and then head home to watch *Beverly Hills 90210*. PHK stood for Pizza Hut and Kelly, our favorite character on the show.

Initially these Wednesday night sessions were basically bitch sessions that we'd spend complaining about some aspect of our jobs. Eventually we started complaining about how ADS was being run, and then finally, what could be done better.

In the summer of 1993 we began exploring the concept of starting our own company and reselling EMTrack, paying ADS a royalty.

On Thanksgiving weekend in 1993 we took a ski trip to Breckenridge, Colorado. A bunch of us went: Bob Durkin and his girlfriend, Jennifer Sax (whom he later married); David Cohen and his girlfriend, Dana McClain (whom he later married and then divorced); Bob's sister, her husband, and me. Before going up to Breckenridge we spent some time in Boulder visiting a friend of mine, Amy Robillard. Little did we know that this trip would later lead to our relocating to Boulder.

The weather while skiing in Breckenridge was the coldest I'd ever experienced in Colorado. I remember that with the windchill it was 40 below. David and Bob still tease me because none of them knew how to ski, and before taking off to ski with Amy I accidentally pointed them in the wrong direction for the lift that went to the top of the mountain. As every skier knows, there are only expert runs at the top of the mountain, not beginner runs. Oops.

The trip to Colorado was significant not only because it provided us with our eventual home, but also because we incorporated within a couple of days of our return.

After many PHK discussions around what we might do, the final straw came when a contact of David's, a company called Reliable Termite and Pest Control, needed some IT consulting. David wanted to run this business through a newly created company, so we got things rolling.

December 7, 1993

I remember the moment we started our business as if it were yesterday. We sat at ADS late at night and used David's CompuServe account to dial into an organization called The Company Corporation, which created companies online for a small fee. We signed in, filled out the online form, and paused when we got to the name. We didn't have one.

On the spot, we brainstormed a list of possible names. One leading contender was Boomtown Enterprises, after a popular song at the time by a group called David and David. Eventually we settled on RightWith, Inc., which is a play on words (say it out loud and think "ink" not "inc.").

At the time we weren't sure what the company would do, only that we wanted to run our own show. It was David's idea; he had always had a goal of starting a company by the age of 30 and being a millionaire by the age of 40.

Although both of us had saved some money, we funded RightWith with $50 each. Neither of us ever articulated it, but we had a strong desire to create something out of nothing. The $100 went into the bank. There were no expenses, no plan, and no company. We just knew that we were tired of having to implement John's vaporware.

The Early RightWith Years

Now that we had a company, one of the first things we did was to get an 800 number and a fancy answering machine called a Friday. The Friday was pretty sophisticated for the $200 we paid for it. It allowed you to choose an employee, "ring their phone" (even though there wasn't one), and let the caller leave a voicemail. Friday would then page the appropriate person so that they could call in and retrieve the message. The machine and the phone line were in the closet of the guest bedroom of my condo in Miami, but all this was done in an effort to appear professional.

RW Inc.

We're right there with you...

RightWith, Inc.
3192 Bird Ave.
Miami, FL 33133
Ph: (800) 4 RIGHTW x 723
or: (800) 474-4489
Fax: (800) 4 RIGHTW
CIS: 75330, 122

David G. Cohen
Partner

Our first business card, with my home address and the phone number, 800-4RIGHTW (for RightWith), that Pinpoint/ZOLL still uses, the answering machine extension, and the CompuServe account number (to send email). David and I both used the title "Partner."

ADS was going through a stranger period than usual. They were in the process of selling the EMTrack intellectual property to a company called RadioSoft, which was owned by EFJohnson, a radio company. ADS would remain the company that outsourced dispatch services and RadioSoft would use the software to help sell more radios. RadioSoft was going to split EMTrack and the call center operations into two different companies, although I'm sure that for John the impetus behind the deal was to get some income to fund expenses, such as payroll.

We saw an opportunity and we seized it. RadioSoft wanted EMTrack but didn't want the EMTrack support function. John wasn't charging customers for EMTrack support, which was something that we often complained about during our PHK sessions, so he was happy to turn over the support responsibility to RightWith, as it helped him with his issue with the RadioSoft people.

So in early 1994 RightWith began charging for EMTrack support, and even improved on it by offering a program for a fee whereby we would do an annual customer visit to make sure everything was running smoothly.

When I reflect back on it, it's important to ask why John would let us run our own company, generate our own support revenue, and take business trips to visit customers while still taking a salary at ADS. John understood people very well and knew that if he stood in the way of our dreams we would leave and pursue them without him. I think he felt that getting some productivity out of us was better than getting none, and that perhaps our efforts to get RightWith going might not pan out and we would return to ADS full time. He fully supported us because he supported career development and happy employees, but he thought that we would fail. Of course, that didn't happen.

So for the first few months, the company that would become Pinpoint did little more than support a half dozen EMTrack accounts at $5,000 per year for each one and do odd contract work for Reliable for considerably less money. We didn't take any salary and just built up the bank account for whatever it was we were going to do next.

Eventually we started thinking about what we could do. For a while we considered reselling EMTrack. We worked up a complete business plan to present to John, in which we would take no ADS salary but would pay ADS half of all EMTrack sales, yet sell, deploy, and support the systems ourselves. We thought that this could be a win for each of us because ADS could make some extra money that they weren't going to see anyway, and David and I could make what we considered to be a very good living on the other 50 percent.

Eventually, though, we realized that EMTrack, a DOS-based system, was soon going to be obsolete. At that time, in early 1994, Windows 3.1 had just come out. Unlike Windows 3.0, it caught on quickly because word processing and other applications were selling Windows versions. The ease of use of Windows and the need for running multiple applications simultaneously was quickly becoming apparent. David and I realized that rather than licensing ADS technology, we should create a Windows version of EMTrack and make it our own. So we scrapped the business plan before showing it to John and changed course.

I don't think John ever had any hard feelings about the fact that we took the knowledge we gained creating EMTrack and used it to our benefit. If he did, he certainly never expressed them. Before RightWith was even an idea, we had talked to John about the concept of creating a Windows version of EMTrack, which we called

Rev III. He wasn't all that interested, since ADS was in the business of providing services through its dispatch centers, not selling software.

The spring of 1994 was a busy time. Once we conceived of this new Windows-based CAD system, which we called RightCAD to match the company name RightWith, things started to move quickly.

> Looking back, I've always found it strange that we started a company without having much of an idea of what the company would do. When I read *Good to Great* by Jim Collins, I noted that one of Jim's theories about what makes great companies is that it's more important to have "the right people on the bus" than knowing what you are going to do. That was certainly the case with us. David and I (and Bob too, although he hadn't officially joined us yet) always saw eye-to-eye and I think we had a great ability to differentiate between a good idea and a bad one.

Moving Away

Just as things got going, we both moved away from Miami. David moved to Phoenix to be near Dana as she attended graduate school. We had spent many PHKs trying to find a way to get Eran to Phoenix. Eran was extremely productive for ADS, but only because David was there to feed him what to do. Without David, Eran would be no use to John. David and Eran were still on ADS' payroll, so we convinced John to have Eran move with David so that David could continue to direct him in ADS' activities.

In Phoenix, David and Eran shared an apartment, although David usually stayed across the street at Dana's. Eran had some odd habits, like keeping all his utensils in plastic bags and wearing the same clothes for six months and then switching to a new set, even though he showered three times a day and was obsessively clean.

While in Phoenix, David and Eran worked on what we thought would be a prototype of RightCAD, but as work progressed it became the real product. It was initially an exercise on David's part to learn the ins and outs of programming in Windows and to implement some of the more difficult concepts, starting with the map software. Eventually David spent most of his time doing the work for John on EMTrack and Eran coded the bulk of the RightCAD application.

We moved the 800 number from my condo's closet in Miami to Phoenix since David could now actually answer the phone, but I tried to do as much support myself as possible, leaving David and Eran more time to work on RightCAD.

Every few months I would visit Phoenix to see the progress that had been made, provide any input I might have, and have long discussions with David about business issues. What those issues were I can't even imagine anymore, since we didn't have any actual business. From the beginning, though, we always got into the minutiae of analyzing how Eran was doing, our relationship with John, and where we thought we were going. This stayed with us throughout our days at Pinpoint, where we had pre-meeting meetings to discuss what we would discuss at meetings.

TransCare

Meanwhile, back at ADS, John had met a guy named Don Strange, who was trying to put together a Wall Street–backed deal in which several ambulance companies in the New York City area would be purchased and consolidated.

John's involvement was in providing the contacts, as most of the initial six TransCare companies were EMTrack users. In the course of getting things going, I became very interested in TransCare. I think John realized that he couldn't keep me at ADS any longer and he helped me get a position as Don's director of technology. In June of 1994, I moved to New York to work for TransCare full time.

Technically I was still living in Miami. Don was based in Dallas, Texas, and had a vision that New York was to be TransCare's first operation, with other rollups planned for other cities. Since I was officially with corporate, I was expected to move to Dallas. Since I knew that eventually RightWith was going to be my full-time job, I convinced Don that I should remain in Miami until New York was done and then move to Dallas, knowing that I would likely be gone by then.

Bob Durkin was living in my townhouse in Miami and Jenn moved in once I left for New York. I would come back from New York every other weekend. Having no roots was hard for me: I used to joke that the question I dreaded most from the person sitting next to me on the plane was, "So where do you live, Miami or New York?" I didn't really live in either place.

TransCare was a fascinating experience for me. Even though it was a startup and only had four employees (Don, a CFO named Sean Cunningham, an executive assistant, and me), they had lined up $80 million of financing from Morgan Stanley, although the financing was conditioned on purchasing a certain critical mass of companies at the same time.

I spent a lot of the time with investment bankers when Don and Sean were putting the deals together with them to purchase each of the companies. In the process I felt that I got a crash course in the Wall Street business environment, meeting with bankers, owners, and sellers and being privy to a lot of negotiations, politics, and power dinners.

I stayed in Long Beach, on Long Island. TransCare had rented an oceanfront apartment near TWC (John Stapleton's company), one of the companies that was to be acquired. I commuted 90 minutes each way into Manhattan by train. Staying in the city until late at night, I'd often joke that I got more sleep on the train than I did in my bed.

I can't begin to describe how crazy a place TransCare was. Laypeople have a view of the ambulance business that isn't always correct. In practice, privately owned ambulance companies are often started up by paramedics with no business experience who happen to be smart and ambitious enough to want more. That, combined with the fact that it's not typically a very profitable business, leads to a lot of cutting corners, cost cutting, and dirty, often illegal, tricks.

I remember a meeting where Sean was doing some due diligence on one of the companies to be acquired, making sure that their business practices were on the up-and-up. Under New York Medicaid rules you could bill Medicaid for tolls that an ambulance or wheelchair van had to pay. Since you bill by the patient, Sean asked the company's owner what he did if several patients were in the van at the time of the toll. The owner replied, quite proudly, that he billed the toll on each of the patients' trips. This was clearly fraud.

One day I was assigned to give a tour to a number of bankers of one of the companies to be acquired that was located in a particularly dangerous area of the South Bronx. In an area where it was recommended that one not stop at red lights, even if it was daylight, they showed up in limos.

Having arrived early to make sure that we were ready for the tour, I found a junkie in the front lobby with three wheelchairs. My conversation with the owner went as follows:

"What's that guy doing?"

"He wants to talk to me. He's selling wheelchairs."

"Oh, can you talk to him soon? I'm not sure the bankers will be impressed."

"Yeah, well, I usually wait half an hour, that way he needs a fix so bad that the price goes down."

"Um, well, ok, whatever. Do what you can."

"You know, the funny thing is that he always shows up right after somebody steals a bunch of our wheelchairs. I think he's selling me my wheelchairs."

Things at TransCare were slow, because it was taking longer than expected to purchase the five ambulance companies. Since my job wouldn't really begin until the consolidation began, I was left with lots of free time.

I spent a lot of time with the owner of TWC, Al Liguori, and his son Mike, who had become a good friend of mine. Al and I discussed all the ins and outs of TransCare and then, out of boredom, we would often play racquetball.

> While still drawing salary from ADS, David and Bob came to New York to deploy EMTrack to what would be the last customer, Midwood Ambulance. They stayed with me at my apartment and still joke that they were working until late at night while I was taking naps on the couch and playing racquetball.

While at TransCare, I got a great lesson in office politics. You couldn't have asked for a more politically charged environment. We were acquiring five companies, each of which was run by someone who had grown the business from the ground up. Each owner/CEO was a headstrong individual, even by New York standards, jockeying for position in the new organization.

I was in a unique position. While everyone else was fighting to have TransCare look like their old organization, I had no vested interest. Consequently, I was viewed by Don as having a good independent opinion and was included in a wide range of the decision making, from uniforms to operational details. It was a great learning experience in the inner workings of the highest level of a relatively large organization.

Eventually, as Pinpoint got going, I would resign my position with TransCare and would be replaced by John Stapleton.

Chapter 3 The Early Years

Funding

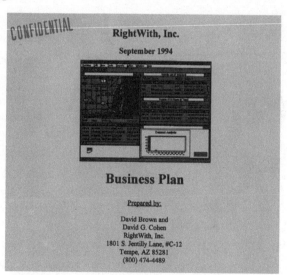

The cover of our business plan. Note the screen cap of the prototype of RightCAD, running in Windows 3.11.

For the year that I was in New York, I spoke to David every day about the details of RightCAD, mostly acting as a sounding board. They would be considered boring conversations now, but back then we were fascinated by the minutiae of how a feature should work, whether we should use ODBC, whether Windows or OS/2 was a better operating system, and whether we should use Access or Btrieve as a database or Microsoft or Borland as a development tool. In addition to doing EMTrack support, I used my free time to do the accounting, pay the bills, write the user manual for RightCAD, and most importantly, write a business plan for RightWith. Among other things, the business plan outlined the need for $100,000 to get things going.

> I remember spending a weekend in the ADS offices in Miami with David and Bob working on 1995–1997 financial projections for the business plan. We created detailed projections of sales, expenses in a number of categories, and whom we would hire when. The process was typical for us in the early days. We'd come in and work hard in a very focused way to do the best job we could. Ultimately, the numbers proved to be accurate within 3 percent.

Once the business plan was completed in September of 1994, I tried to find someone to lend us the $100K. RightWith had its bank account in Miami, so I took a day off from TransCare and flew to Miami to make my pitch. The banker I spoke to was friendly and polite, but in the end she explained that the bank couldn't lend money to a company that had no track record of success. She recommended that I try the Small Business Administration (SBA), a government agency that helps small companies get started. It was my first experience of what I had already heard but never fully realized: banks only lend money to people who don't need it.

My pitch to the SBA went much the same way as my pitch to the bank. Without any track record, we were too small, even by SBA standards. They weren't interested.

My third pitch was to a company called AID Ambulance in Indianapolis. AID was a current EMTrack user and had complained to David and me about ADS' lack of support for improving the product. Rick Archer was the director of communications for AID and our main point of contact for EMTrack support. I arranged to go to Pittsburgh for that year's APCO industry trade show, which Rick was attending. We sat down face-to-face and I outlined our ideas for RightWith. Rick liked our ideas and promised to take the business plan to AID's CEO, Paul Smith, and the owners, Paul and Nancy Herriter.

The folks at AID liked the business plan enough that they asked David and me to come to Indianapolis to show what we had done so far and discuss the plan in greater detail. At that time, RightCAD was really just a prototype with some dispatch screens but no ability to enter a new call. We had created the prototype using a Btrieve database, the same one that EMTrack used. Our idea for the demo was that we would install a version of RightCAD that could read all of AID's live data in the EMTrack system. So we immediately set out to prepare the best possible demo.

The timing of the demo couldn't have been worse from the perspective of my current job. TransCare had chosen the same day to announce to all five companies that they were going to be acquired and things were pretty crazy around the office. That evening there was to be a dinner for all mid-level managers to introduce all the new players at TransCare, including me.

I never did tell anyone at TransCare that I was going out of town. Site A thought I was going to Site B and Site B thought I was going to Site A. During the demo I was paged by my boss and I found a moment to call him back. He never did know that I wasn't in New York. Meanwhile, the timing was tight, but I knew that I could make the dinner. I even parked my car at the airport facing the exit in the best possible spot to dash to the dinner after I landed. Fortunately, my flight wasn't delayed, I changed out of my suit into casual dinner clothes in the car, and I was only 15 minutes late to the dinner. Only John Stapleton, one of the TransCare midlevel managers, knew the true story.

The meeting at AID went great. The software prototype, worked on by David and Eran until the eleventh hour, performed flawlessly. By the end of the meeting, the CEO of AID was selling it to the owners for us. He said, "You know, the beauty of this is that it's a Windows program. I've never seen it before, but I can pretty much guess that like all other Windows programs it has an option that says About under the Help menu." Fortunately, we were able to show that this was true.

It was a stroke of genius, or perhaps luck, to have RightCAD run on AID's live Btrieve database. Once the folks at AID saw their data, their calls, and their vehicles showing up in RightCAD, their eyes lit up. Even though there were several components missing that would make it workable, they understood what it would look like when it did work.

The demo was successful enough that AID asked us to come back to talk about a deal. By the end of this second visit we had a commitment from AID to give us our funding. We had gone into the meeting willing to give them up to 10 percent ownership in the company and were ecstatic to end up with an agreement to simply pay back the loan with interest out of future sales and pay an ongoing royalty of 2.5 percent. Little did we know that this agreement would haunt us in our subsequent sale to ZOLL.

Although the agreement in principle was done on the spot, it took many months to get to a legal contract. When we saw the first draft, we were extremely excited, because we skipped right to the part where they were to give us the $100,000, and it was there! Of course, the contract had a number of other heinous provisions that protected AID if things went wrong. It's a good thing they didn't, because David and I would probably still be paying off that loan personally and AID would have complete rights to the RightCAD source code.

Paul Smith, the CEO, was also an attorney and drafted the documents himself. We got a crash course in legalese and read and commented on the contract ourselves. In the end, before signing, we showed the contract to an attorney, but not understanding our business, he wasn't much help. The deal was as follows:

- AID was to lend us $100,000, payable in 12 monthly payments of $8,333.33 each. We had shown in our business plan that we needed 10 payments of $10,000 in order to meet our cash-flow needs, but we figured their offer was good enough. As it turned out, the difference almost killed us, as we almost ran out of cash.
- We would pay back $125,000 (the $100,000 plus interest) at a rate of 5 percent of all RightWith sales made after the full $100,000 had been paid to us.
- After the $125,000 was paid off, we would pay AID a royalty of 2.5 percent of sales, and 2 percent of sales over $10 million. When we made the verbal agreement we had asked for the royalty rate to be reduced over time and agreed on the $10 million cap. When the first draft of the contract came back to us, the cap was $10 million per year, meaning that the rate started over at 2.5 percent at the beginning of each year. Although we realized that we hadn't made that

clear one way or the other in our initial discussions, we were so worried about jeopardizing the $100,000 that we didn't even bring up that point. Later this royalty turned into a lot of money, until ZOLL finally reached a deal with Rural/Metro, which had bought AID, to buy them out of the contract for $750,000.

- AID would get to use the RightCAD software for free.
- The biggest kicker at the time was that David and I would have to personally guarantee the $125,000. That meant that if RightWith didn't pay it back we would have to, out of our future earnings or personal assets. This personal guarantee weighed on us for a long time and we were very relieved when the $125,000 finally got paid off in April of 1998.

In the end, none of the clauses would come back to haunt us except the 2.5 percent ongoing royalty, which we should have negotiated down. We worried about all the little details if things went wrong, but forgot about the big detail if things went right.

Overall it was a great deal for us. We got our startup capital without having to give up ownership in the company. While we had to personally guarantee a loan, we figured that was to be expected in a startup situation. In hindsight, we probably should have negotiated down the royalty, but if it had been a deal breaker, it would have been worth leaving in. Ultimately, we got the company going and I'm not sure how we would have if it hadn't been for AID.

To this day, I am extremely grateful to Jack and Nancy Herriter for believing in this two-man company and putting up the money to get us going. The sad part is that I never spoke to them again after our presentation and never got the opportunity to thank them. In 1996 they sold AID Ambulance to Rural/Metro, a consolidator similar to, but much larger than, TransCare. I have no idea what ever became of them.

When AID sold their company to Rural/Metro, we realized that our contract had a clause that allowed them unlimited use of the system. We suddenly were very worried that this would now mean that Rural/Metro could use RightCAD in their operations nationwide for free. We "sort of" came to an agreement that they could only use it in the state of Indiana, but this situation is an example of why you want a good attorney reviewing your contracts.

The path to the "sort of" agreement was messy. A Rural/Metro attorney faxed us a standard assignment form that Rural/Metro was taking over the contract from AID. Before signing the assignment, we added in "Indiana" as a change. They never accepted the change, sent it back to us, or discussed it in any way until we needed them to sign a document in our sale to ZOLL. John Banas, their new corporate attorney, caught the fact that they might be entitled to use the software nationwide for free. When I pointed out the Indiana clause, he said, "Yes, but we didn't accept that." I said that if they didn't accept that, there was no assignment of the contract, so they couldn't use the software at all. Fortunately, John liked me and left it at that.

I have mixed feelings about starting a company on so little cash. The business plan we wrote was certainly a best-case scenario with no margin for error. It's easy to look back and say that this forced us to make it work, but there were plenty of events I can point to that would have caused us to go bankrupt had luck not played in our favor.

While we could have made things happen faster had we had millions in funding, I believe that spending within your means is a great lesson to learn for any business leader. Reflecting back, I wish we had asked for $150,000 instead of $100,000, as the extra $50,000, while a small amount, would have made a big difference for us.

RightWith's First Office

David and I standing in front of our first office, the "bomb shelter" at 1801 S. Jentilly Lane, #C-12, in Tempe, Arizona. It had RightWith, Inc. on the door and we were very proud.

Once the contract was signed, the race was on to get a working product to AID. The business plan called for this to be done by April 1995 and any delay would cause us to run out of cash.

David and Eran officially left ADS and went on the RightWith payroll on September 15, 1994. Technically, the contract wasn't signed until January, but we risked it since we felt comfortable that the contract would get done. At the time we had about $6,000 in the bank, almost enough to get us to January. It was our first big risk, to have David and Eran on payroll. Up to that point we only had revenue from the EMTrack support customers and virtually no expenses other than the cost of the 800 number and some travel costs.

At the time we offered Eran a very low salary and a royalty on future sales. That royalty grew and grew over the years until we negotiated a new agreement with Eran just prior to the sale to ZOLL. We were concerned that ZOLL wouldn't be interested in buying a company that had a royalty going to AID and one going to one of its programmers.

We rented a cheap office on Jentilly Lane in Tempe, Arizona, which we referred to as the "bomb shelter" since the ceiling and walls were made of concrete. It was two offices and was enough room for David and Eran. Rent was $264 a month for 300 square feet.

David and Eran worked day and night to get the product done. We had a couple of 486 computers that David and Eran programmed on, but they weren't very fast, so we bought a brand-new Pentium 70 MHz for $3,500. Because we could

Eran Shay at his desk in the bomb shelter, programming RightCAD on a 286.

only afford one new computer, David worked from 7 a.m. to 7 p.m. and Eran worked from 7 p.m. to 7 a.m. so that we could make the best use of the fast machine.

Preparing for Beta

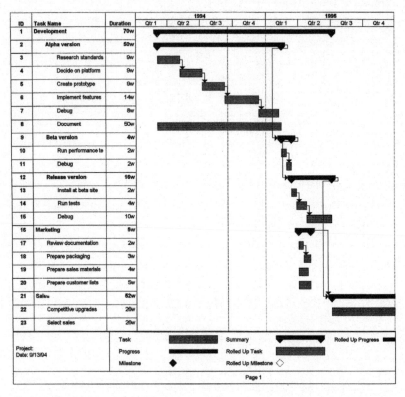

ID	Task Name	Duration	1994				1995			
			Qtr 1	Qtr 2	Qtr 3	Qtr 4	Qtr 1	Qtr 2	Qtr 3	Qtr 4
1	Development	70w								
2	Alpha version	50w								
3	Research standards	9w								
4	Decide on platform	9w								
5	Create prototype	9w								
6	Implement features	14w								
7	Debug	8w								
8	Document	50w								
9	Beta version	4w								
10	Run performance te	2w								
11	Debug	2w								
12	Release version	16w								
13	Install at beta site	2w								
14	Run tests	4w								
15	Debug	10w								
16	Marketing	5w								
17	Review documentation	2w								
18	Prepare packaging	3w								
19	Prepare sales materials	4w								
20	Prepare customer lists	5w								
21	Sales	52w								
22	Competitive upgrades	26w								
23	Select sales	26w								

Project:
Date: 9/13/94

Task		Summary		Rolled Up Progress
Progress		Rolled Up Task		
Milestone	◆	Rolled Up Milestone ◇		

Page 1

Our project plan for rolling out RightCAD. We completed it on schedule.

From the beginning we've always said that our system was designed from the ground up to run on Windows 95, but that simply isn't true. Development of RightCAD began as a project in early 1994. Really, we were just seeing what could be done with maps in a Windows 3.11 environment. The code David wrote to display the maps grew over time to include dispatch modules and a call-taking screen and eventually became RightCAD.

In 1994 Windows was just beginning to be accepted as a preferred solution for applications. Windows 3.0 had been considered more of a curiosity, but Windows 3.11 applications such as WordPerfect and Lotus finally had Windows versions that seemed to work as well as or better than their DOS counterparts.

As the features in RightCAD increased, so did the load on the computer's resources. I remember a critical day in early 1995, just a few weeks from our scheduled delivery date. David called me to let me know that the system had gotten too big and wouldn't run anymore. He decided to get a subscription to a Microsoft developer program called MSDN (Microsoft Developer Network), which would give him an advance copy of their upcoming operating system, code-named "Chicago." Fortunately, RightCAD worked fine on Chicago. We made the operating system switch and never looked back. Chicago would eventually be renamed Windows 95.

It's a good thing RightCAD ran on Windows 95, because at this point we were committed. David and Eran were working for RightWith full time and Bob and I had both quit our jobs. We were well underway to coming together to live in the same city after the system was installed. We were finally going to be a real company and it's a good thing that we had a product that had a chance of working!

This was not a common occurrence in the early days. There were plenty of times, including during the beta installation, that we thought there was no way that we would ever get the software working. Somehow, though, David and Eran would always come up with a miracle solution and we'd be on our way again. We simply refused to give up.

Choosing Where to Live

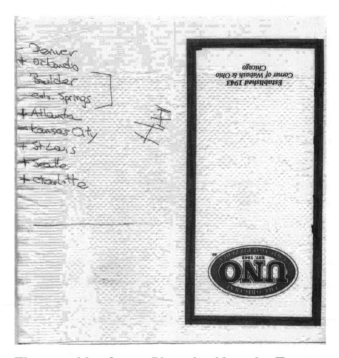

The napkin from Pizzeria Uno in Tempe, Arizona, we used to decide where we would live.

In early 1995 we knew that we were going to make a go of Pinpoint, but David and Eran were living in Phoenix, I was living in New York, and Bob, who by then we knew was going to join us, was living in Miami. None of us felt that we wanted to stay where we were, and we knew that if this were to work, we'd all have to be living in the same place.

During one of my trips to Phoenix in early 1995, we sat down for dinner at a Pizzeria Uno to decide where that place would be. Present were David, Dana, Eran, and myself. Dana's friend Christie was there for moral support and we had input from Bob in advance. The decision was supposed to be 50 percent personal and 50 percent business, but I've always said that it was more like 98 percent personal and 2 percent business.

On a napkin, we wrote out all the possibilities. Everyone got to nominate a place that interested them, and the cities nominated were Denver, Orlando, Boulder, Colorado Springs, Atlanta, Kansas City, St. Louis, Seattle, and Charlotte. Next, each of us could veto other people's suggestions that we didn't like. Boulder was the only city that wasn't eliminated by veto, so we decided to move there.

> The method of offering a suggestion and then having a veto was a technique that David and I liked a lot. For the next 10 years we would use it as a method to decide where we would go to lunch.

The 0th User Conference

While at ADS, David had started the tradition of having EMTrack user conferences at ADS' offices in Miami each year. In March 1995 RightWith was doing all of the EMTrack support, so we held the user conference, although it was still at ADS's offices. We used the opportunity to show off our latest version of RightCAD, which we explained to customers would be a Windows version of EMTrack. With only a month to go before we were scheduled to take AID live on the product, you would think we would have been able to demo the product, but it was a complete failure and kept crashing.

While there were only a half dozen or so EMTrack customers in attendance, this would be the first version of a yearly user conference Pinpoint would hold in Colorado. Somehow when numbering them we neglected to count the Miami conference, perhaps because we didn't want to remember it. In 2003, at my last Summit, as the Colorado user conferences were called, there were more than 280 customers. By 2013, there were more than 700.

Chapter 4 Becoming a Real Company

From RightWith to Pinpoint Technologies

We had known for a while that RightWith, which had originated as a joke, couldn't stick if we were going to be a real company. However, we couldn't come up with a name that we liked and agonized over it for months.

On one of my trips to Phoenix, a friend of Dana's, Christie Jenks, came up with the idea of Pinpoint Technologies, with the tagline "We put your fleet on the map." She even used her computer to design the font and had a little pin over one of the *I*s.

The name sounded okay, but we agonized some more. David was concerned that everyone would call us "Pinheads." We even contemplated reserving the 800 number 1-800-PIN-HEAD to head people off at the pass. In the end we didn't come up with anything better and Pinpoint grew on us. Eventually, we changed the name. We continued to use the tagline, font, and pin designed by Christie for many years.

Moving to Boulder

In March 1995 I had just finished my last day at Trans-Care and flew out to Boulder for two days to find an apartment. Then I flew to Miami to help host the disastrous 0th user conference. The following day, I drove up to Orlando to attend Bob's wedding and I left that night to drive to Colorado.

I spent the first week in Boulder by myself. My job was to find an office and I chose the cheapest one I could find. It had brown shag carpeting, air conditioning that didn't work (although we didn't know that yet), and a landlord named Vern who lived illegally in his office next door. It was about 800 square feet and the rent was $795 per month.

Bob and Jenn came out a week later, after a quick honeymoon in Cancun. Jenn stayed in my apartment while looking for a place for her and Bob, while he jumped on a plane with me to go to Phoenix to help prepare for beta.

Bob and I spent one week in Phoenix, helping to quality test the RightCAD product in preparation for our trip to Indianapolis. Our plan was to solve as much as we could in Phoenix and then to spend two weeks installing the software in Indianapolis. If more time was required to get AID live, Bob and I would alternate weeks until AID was up and running successfully. We hoped that this wouldn't be necessary because we didn't have the money to fly back and forth or to stay in hotels.

Beta

Bob Durkin (left) and I going over lists of bugs in Rick Archer's office at AID Ambulance in Indianapolis.

RightCAD running in a live environment for the first time, April 1995 in Indianapolis.

Bob and I had a bit of a surprise in Phoenix, as the software had a lot of problems. There was a long list of bugs, in addition to calls not being saved correctly. Furthermore, the system was very slow and there was no functionality to set up the vehicles' and crew members' names without going directly into the database.

We refused to give up. This time we created an assembly-line environment. Bob and I found the problems and documented them on lists. David took the lists, split them with Eran, and made the fixes. Bob and I then tested the fixes and crossed the items off. This went on nonstop for the whole week.

Bob and I then flew to Indianapolis to install the product. We had little money, so we shared a room in the cheapest place we could find, in an apartment complex far from the office. AID arranged to have an ambulance pick us up each morning and take us back each night so that we wouldn't have to pay for a rental car. We worked such long hours that we took turns sleeping in the stretcher on the way to and from the office.

The first thing we did when we arrived was to set up a Microsoft Mail server so that we could use email to communicate with David. In April 1995 email and the Internet weren't mainstream, and we needed to hook up a machine to a dedicated phone line so it could make calls back and forth with a similar machine in Phoenix.

Although we fixed a lot of the problems while in Phoenix, we didn't fix them all. The assembly-line environment continued while we were in Indianapolis, with extra problems found by the AID staff, such as the system taking more than three minutes to save a call, which wasn't acceptable in a 911 environment. We made steady progress until the software was stable enough to take the customer live. We did so, on schedule, at midnight on April 16, 1995.

After that, we relaxed a bit. Bob returned to Boulder to be with his new bride and I stayed in Indianapolis for another week, reporting additional problems to David and making sure that everything was okay. Then I too returned to Boulder.

> We were amazed at how easy it was to transition to RightCAD. The system is so easy to use that our call takers and dispatchers picked it up right away and were immediately more productive. And for managers like me, the reporting mechanisms are so comprehensive that I can immediately get more information about my operation.
>
> —Rick Archer, director of dispatch operations for AID Ambulance, in an April 1995 endorsement obviously written by us

Pinpoint's Second Office

Now that AID was up and running there were a lot of administrative matters to take care of. For one, we had settled on Pinpoint Technologies as the company name and we had to officially change it. We got ourselves set up in the office I had found prior to going to Phoenix and Indianapolis, bought a phone system and some furniture, and settled into our new home. Bob and I officially went on the payroll on May 1, 1995.

David Cohen and I shared the largest office, with a view of the mountains (mostly obscured by a Target), and Bob had a small office in the front. The big entry room was shared by Eran and our receptionist, Zebeth. When John Stapleton joined us, he set up just outside the bathroom.

David Cohen in front of our first Boulder office, at 2111 30th Street, Suite M—the one with the shag carpeting and the landlord named Vern. The sign over the window is the original design by Christie Jenks, complete with pin.

Everything in the office was brown, including the shag carpet. Although it was supposedly air conditioned, it was an old system that couldn't keep up. So we had a fan and made frequent trips to Target to buy drinks. This wasn't an environment in which to dress up, so we wore shorts, T-shirts, and sandals to work.

David and Eran Arrive from Phoenix

A couple of weeks after we moved into our office, David and Eran arrived from Phoenix. They had packed all the office belongings along with their personal stuff in a U-Haul and had driven to Boulder. As we unpacked the computers and other office equipment, we discovered that the box that housed the server was all wet. That server had all our source code on it and we stupidly had no backup. David had placed the small refrigerator he kept in the Phoenix office on top of the server box, and it had defrosted and leaked in transit.

By some miracle, David had had the foresight to pack the server in a plastic bag before putting it in the box. Fortunately, it was dry and worked just fine.

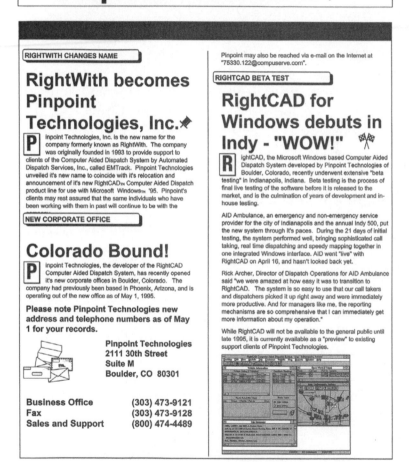

Pinpoint Bulletin May '95

RIGHTWITH CHANGES NAME

RightWith becomes Pinpoint Technologies, Inc.

Pinpoint Technologies, Inc. is the new name for the company formerly known as RightWith. The company was originally founded in 1993 to provide support to clients of the Computer Aided Dispatch System by Automated Dispatch Services, Inc., called EMTrack. Pinpoint Technologies unveiled it's new name to coincide with it's relocation and announcement of it's new RightCAD™ Computer Aided Dispatch product line for use with Microsoft Windows™ '95. Pinpoint's clients may rest assured that the same individuals who have been working with them in past will continue to be with the

NEW CORPORATE OFFICE

Colorado Bound!

Pinpoint Technologies, the developer of the RightCAD Computer Aided Dispatch System, has recently opened it's new corporate offices in Boulder, Colorado. The company had previously been based in Phoenix, Arizona, and is operating out of the new office as of May 1, 1995.

Please note Pinpoint Technologies new address and telephone numbers as of May 1 for your records.

Pinpoint Technologies
2111 30th Street
Suite M
Boulder, CO 80301

Business Office	(303) 473-9121
Fax	(303) 473-9128
Sales and Support	(800) 474-4489

Pinpoint may also be reached via e-mail on the Internet at "75330.122@compuserve.com".

RIGHTCAD BETA TEST

RightCAD for Windows debuts in Indy - "WOW!"

RightCAD, the Microsoft Windows based Computer Aided Dispatch System developed by Pinpoint Technologies of Boulder, Colorado, recently underwent extensive "beta testing" in Indianapolis, Indiana. Beta testing is the process of final live testing of the software before it is released to the market, and is the culmination of years of development and in-house testing.

AID Ambulance, an emergency and non-emergency service provider for the city of Indianapolis and the annual Indy 500, put the new system through it's paces. During the 21 days of initial testing, the system performed well, bringing sophisticated call taking, real time dispatching and speedy mapping together in one integrated Windows interface. AID went "live" with RightCAD on April 16, and hasn't looked back yet.

Rick Archer, Director of Dispatch Operations for AID Ambulance said "we were amazed at how easy it was to transition to RightCAD. The system is so easy to use that our call takers and dispatchers picked it up right away and were immediately more productive. And for managers like me, the reporting mechanisms are so comprehensive that I can immediately get more information about my operation."

While RightCAD will not be available to the general public until late 1995, it is currently available as a "preview" to existing support clients of Pinpoint Technologies.

From its earliest days, Pinpoint produced a newsletter called *To the Point*. This early edition talks about our name change, our move to Colorado, and our successful installation at AID.

Indy 500, Reliable, and David's Wedding

In late May, David and I accepted an invitation from AID to attend the Indianapolis 500. For the previous several years, AID had provided ambulance service for the race car event. To get us on the field, David and I had to dress in bright yellow jumpsuits and help out. At the beginning of the race we were assigned to watch the spectator stands, where a fan in the last row had been decapitated the previous year by flying debris from a crash.

After the race, we drove to Hannibal, Missouri, where David was getting married the following week. With extra time before the wedding, David and I did some on-site consulting for our first client, Reliable Termite and Pest Control, which was located nearby. We pulled cable and tried to get their server fixed but basically had no idea why we were there.

Bob Durkin Becomes a Partner

Bob knew about our plans for RightWith and Pinpoint from the very beginning but was appropriately skeptical about our ability to get funding. While we had included him on our business plan, his name was really there only as a placeholder because Bob hadn't made up his mind to work at the company. It wasn't until after the contract with AID was signed in January 1995 that he decided to join.

From the very beginning Bob had expressed a desire to have equity in the company. However, we'd never worked out the specifics. We had talked to Bob about coming onboard in a sales capacity and getting a commission on sales. Bob had said, "Sure, but I'd like the option to forgo some of the commission and buy some stock instead." That was it. We agreed, not really sure that things were going to work out. Besides, Bob was a friend, so we were sure that we could figure out something that was fair. Looking back, we should have worked out the details of that deal, in writing, on the spot.

Now that we were all in Boulder, we had to decide what was fair. What percentage of the company would Bob own? Would he have to pay for it? While this conversation potentially had disaster written all over it, we were very lucky. David, Bob, and I went back and forth a few times and worked it out, although not until May 1996, a year after we had moved to Boulder.

Getting AID Right

AID went live in April and we didn't sell our next system until August. But in the interim period, all three of us were busy all of the time. David and I primarily supported AID, adding critical features, fixing problems, and stabilizing the system. This went on and on, in an iterative fashion, for months.

This was a critical period for us. While we had delivered a product to AID that worked well enough to be usable, it would not be well accepted by future customers. So while Bob worked on sales, I talked to AID, and David and Eran programmed the features that they needed. We did this all day every day.

Our First Sale

We knew that it would be almost impossible to sell a system if we didn't have a reference site. As important as it was to get the money from AID, it was equally important that they were our first customer. What we didn't anticipate was how difficult it would be to get our second one.

Bob was in charge of sales and had a two-pronged approach to selling our first version of RightCAD. We began by calling on all the other EMTrack users, since we already knew them and they trusted us. The vast majority of these users were in the New York area and we concentrated on them. Unfortunately, at the same time ambulance companies in New York were under tight scrutiny for the trips that they billed to Medicare. Several had been caught billing fraudulent trips and had been assessed huge fines in the tens of millions of dollars. Even the companies that weren't fined clamped down on the types of trips they were running, thereby losing revenue. As one ambulance company owner told us, "The gravy train is over." In this climate, buying updated software systems wasn't a priority, even though we were offering a hefty discount to EMTrack users.

Bob's second strategy was to cold-call local Colorado ambulance services. Most of these companies, however, had been bought up in recent years by the biggest of the consolidators, AMR. The only company we could find that showed even the slightest interest was Columbine Ambulance Service. As time went on and we became more desperate, we kept lowering our price to Columbine. In the end, I believe that we offered them a system for free so that we could have a local reference site. All they had to do was buy the computer that RightCAD would run on. They still said, "No thanks!"

Meanwhile, I stayed in touch with Don Strange, the CEO of TransCare. Don liked me very much but believed that you were "in or out." That meant that once I left the company, he didn't really want to deal with me.

Fortunately for us, however, TransCare purchased a company in Pittsburgh in August 1995. As part of his deal with John Shermyen, Don had an unlimited license to EMTrack at no charge. He wanted to install it in Pittsburgh so he could use it the same way it was used in the New York operation, but felt that I would do a better job than ADS installing the system and training the users. I made Don an offer he couldn't refuse: we could either install EMTrack and train his operation on it for $20,000, or we could sell him a complete RightCAD system for $25,000 (an 80 percent discount). He bought RightCAD.

Bob and I arrived in Pittsburgh to install RightCAD on August 25, 1995, the day after the official release date of Windows 95. TransCare staff had to go to the store to pick up copies for their computers.

Installing EMTrack and RightCAD had historically been a two-man job, but with TransCare we experimented with using just one person. Bob helped out a bit at first, but then took days off to do demos and to try to win more business while I completed the training. This turned out to be a very successful approach.

Our First Trade Show

We returned from our first paying customer feeling flush with money. We had used the $12,500 deposit to pay off our bills and we had another $12,500 to cover an upcoming $5,000 payroll, leaving us around $7,500 in the bank. We had arrived.

Almost immediately, David thought we should use the money to attend AAA, at the time the biggest trade show for the ambulance industry, which was being held at the MGM Grand in Las Vegas in November. We quickly calculated that it would cost us about $14,000 to rent a space, a booth, create some signage, and fly to Las Vegas. Close enough, we figured, and we decided to go. So much for our $7,500.

We really had no choice but to go to the show. It was November 1995, and in another month our monthly checks from AID would end. Sales prospects were poor and the EMTrack upgrade strategy was not working. We needed a way to find new customers, and fast.

All three of us switched into marketing mode. We created as many materials as we could for as little as possible. Bob designed a brochure in Word (we didn't know at the time that word processors are terrible for laying out graphics, and he had a hard time). We created a concept called "RightCAD in a box" to illustrate one of our biggest competitive advantages: that the software was off the shelf and didn't need to be customized for each customer. David created what was probably the cheesiest promotional video ever recorded. We wanted to display the video on a computer screen, because that wasn't commonplace in 1995, and we thought it would bring people by our booth. Finally, we hooked up a video camera so people walking by our booth could see themselves on a computer screen.

At the show, David, Bob, and I had a standard rule for answering customers' questions: we would double everything. So if they asked how many customers we had, the answer was four, not two. If they asked how many employees we had, we had 10. We figured that way we would be consistent and wouldn't get caught in a lie.

We knew that the $14,000 invested would be worth it if we could sell just one system. What we didn't know is that customers rarely sign up at trade shows. Luckily, Bowers Ambulance, a progressive ambulance service in Long Beach, California, was in attendance. Bob Bowers was specifically looking for a good CAD system and liked what he saw in our system.

He was a little worried about the size of our company. Late one evening on the show floor, when we said that we provided support 24 hours a day, seven days a week, he said, "Prove it to me, what's the number?" I wasn't worried about giving him the number. I hadn't lied. The problem was that I was the one who was on call. I didn't think he'd be impressed that the guy who was selling him the system was also the guy whose beeper went off. I didn't want him to know that the whole company was at the trade show. So as David distracted him, I tried to give my pager to Bob, but it didn't work out. My pager went off. I was embarrassed, but thankfully, Bowers was satisfied. He bought the system at the show—one of three customers that I can remember in the history of Pinpoint who purchased at a trade show. We had only about $700 in the bank, so we deposited Bowers' down payment right away.

Zebeth Parks, the Voice of RightCAD

In September of 1995, just before going to the AAA trade show in Las Vegas, we decided to hire a receptionist, mostly in an effort to appear more professional. We hired a great woman named Zebeth Parks as the fifth Pinpoint employee.

> Zebeth was a little nervous about being left in the office alone with Eran while David, Bob, and I went to AAA. After we got back, she told us that she had to put a poster over the tiny area between two dividers that hid Eran's desk from her view. She said it freaked her out to see his eyeball constantly peering through the crack at her.

We let Zebeth go in mid-1997 when Jennifer Jones came onboard, but it was a shortsighted move to save money. Zebeth was a great employee and we should have found a way to keep her.

Zebeth's enduring legacy is that from the beginning, she did all the voice recordings for Pinpoint's phone system and for the recorded voice prompts within RightCAD. After her days at Pinpoint were over, we kept in touch and she continued to come in to make additional recordings.

John Stapleton Arrives

I think that one of John Shermyen's greatest strengths was recognizing great people for the job at hand. John, a great idea guy, really needed David, Bob, and me to implement the ideas he dreamed up.

We tried to do the same at Pinpoint and recognized that John Stapleton, a dispatch manager at TWC in New York, was cut out for more. From the early days of my time at Trans-Care, we had talked to him about the possibility of joining us at Pinpoint. So as I was leaving and John was getting ready to take over my job at TransCare, we made him a great pitch. Come out to Boulder, run our support department (which at the beginning meant "do all the support"), and we'll pay you $30,000 a year. Amazingly, John accepted.

In the early days of Pinpoint, we recruited at amazingly low salaries. We did this by using the lure of working for a small startup that was going places. We offered no equity but offered an opportunity for career growth in a very exciting, energy-charged environment.

John was the first of many employees we would recruit from the industry and relocate to Colorado. I believe that the depth of knowledge we had in the form of dispatchers, billing managers, and paramedics helped propel Pinpoint to a leadership position.

John left New York in January 1996 with all of his worldly belongings packed into a U-Haul truck, after being delayed a few days due to a major snowstorm. We hadn't shared with John just how tight our finances were, and he might not have accepted the position had he known that we only had $700 in the bank at the time we signed up Bowers. We had agreed to pay for what we thought would be John's modest moving expenses and were shocked to see him arrive in one of the largest U-Haul trucks available, with his belongings barely covering the floor. This was a $2,000 expense that we didn't really think we could afford at a time when we were still agonizing about whether we could afford to buy a $400 printer. We paid the expense, of course, and tried not to let our concern show too much.

Pinpoint's Culture

Before he accepted the position, John came out to Colorado to visit and stayed at my small apartment. I heard him describing Pinpoint to a friend on the phone, "You wouldn't believe it: I'm the best-dressed guy here, because even though I'm wearing shorts, my shirt has a collar."

From the beginning, we ran the office as if it were our living room. We wanted the office to be a place that was comfortable and fun to work. None of us had ever put a lot of stock into appearances, and work became our life while our life invaded our work. As John put it to another friend later on, "It's kind of weird. When we go out, we always wind up talking about work. But then again, we're always laughing at work."

We made very little distinction between work and play. We were all friends and we all did things together outside of working hours. We had regular Thursday night TV viewings, where we would take turns hosting dinner and watching *Friends, ER*, and whatever miscellaneous shows NBC ran in between. We also had regular Friday night outings to the James, a local Irish pub.

For years we joked that the only dress code at Pinpoint was "underwear on the inside." This came from the fact that one of our early employees, Andy Cutright, had a habit of wearing sweatpants with boxer shorts on top. This casual-dress-code-to-the-extreme survived until the day I left. It was great to be able to go into the office in shorts and sandals, and I believe that it was a great way to draw and retain employees as well.

> Andy Cutright was a character. Hired as a programmer in January 1996, Andy would routinely come in to work in a Santa-like hat that was always bouncing around. In the early days we used to joke that working at Pinpoint was like an episode of Seinfeld, with Andy as Kramer. In many ways, Andy's dress code and habit of yelling out for no particular reason contributed to Pinpoint's laid-back culture.

We tried to keep the organizational structure as flat as possible. While people had bosses and were accountable to them, we didn't want management at a different class level. One tradition that grew out of this was what we called the Pinpoint Salute. Instituted by Bob Durkin, the Pinpoint Salute consisted of giving the bird to any other employee who happened to walk by, at any time.

Years later, when we were much bigger, I was walking by our conference room, where I could see that Al Thompson and our HR director, Cindy Treloar, were interviewing a job applicant. Because the candidate had his back to me, I gave Al and Cindy the Salute. From reflex, Al shot one right back at me, in full view of the candidate. I can only imagine what the candidate thought. I did notice a look of terror in Cindy's eyes.

Our Second Sale

Pinpoint Technologies
We put your fleet on the map.

David Brown
Vice-President, Business Development

Pinpoint Technologies, Inc.
2111 30th St, Suite M   *(303) 473-9121 x104*
Boulder, CO 80301   *Fax: (303) 473-9128*

The first Pinpoint business card, printed at Kinko's. Everyone was a director or a VP.

One of John's first tasks was to provide me with assistance in installing RightCAD for our second sale, Bowers Ambulance. With some brief training at the office, we set off to California to deploy for the customer. John started off a little skeptical because he saw how often RightCAD crashed compared to the rock-solid stability of EMTrack. In addition, we were installing the software on the brand-new Windows 95, instead of the older Windows 3.1. John's famous comment was "I'm still not sold on this Windows 95 thing."

> John arrived at Bowers before I did. When he handed a business card that said "Director of Support" to Bowers' arrogant general manager, his first comment was "Is there anyone at Pinpoint that isn't a director or VP?" Other than Eran and Zebeth, the answer was no.

The Bowers install was almost a disaster. The software worked okay, but for some reason, the database that we were using at the time, Access 2.0, kept corrupting and crashing. Of course, when the database crashes and users can't use a CAD product, this is a very bad thing when you are dispatching ambulances. This happened day after day for weeks. We became very good at rebuilding the data and getting them back online quickly. This could happen at any time of the day or night, so these were rough times. Fortunately, no data was ever lost and under the circumstances the customer was extremely tolerant. I think he saw that we were working as hard as possible to fix the problem. There were plenty of times when I spoke to Bob Bowers at 3 a.m., once even on New Year's Eve.

> Eventually, in 1997, we changed the database to SQL Server, as too many customers had experienced the same problems as Bowers, although none as frequently. For any IT guy now, the choice to use Access rather than SQL seems crazy. SQL is the product designed for applications with a large number of transactions, like RightCAD. In 1995, though, Microsoft SQL was on version 4.2 and was an unstable and virtually unknown product. It wasn't until the release of version 6.0 that the platform became viable.

The Bowers install was made even more complicated because it required an interface that moved information between RightCAD and their billing vendor, Ambpac. Somehow Duncan, the president of Ambpac, heard my name and called me up, refusing to allow an interface until I settled the debt that he claimed he had with John Shermyen, with whom he had subcontracted many years earlier. I had a difficult time convincing him that Pinpoint was a separate company from ADS. Duncan said things like, "I know John had you guys locked up, I saw your employment agreements." Unfortunately, Duncan was another victim of an excellent John Shermyen sales job, as no such agreements existed. Duncan finally relented under pressure from Bowers and let the interface move forward.

Clemente, RAM, and Jennifer Jones

Our first install was at AID Ambulance in April 1995. Our first paying customer was TransCare Pennsylvania in August 1995. Our second customer was Bowers Ambulance in November 1995 and our third was Clemente-McKay Ambulance in December 1995.

We met Clemente through TransCare Pennsylvania's billing vendor, a company called RAM Software Systems. RAM had a number of billing customers in the area, many of whom were interested in a dispatch system. Clemente was another billing customer of RAM's and they had already taken money from Clemente to create a dispatch system for them, but they had trouble getting it up and running. RAM's president, Brian McIntyre, and I, helped by a consultant who worked at Clemente named Lori Fuzo, entered into a very informal agreement whereby they could sell our RightCAD system to their customers and receive a portion of the proceeds. We called the agreement a six-month trial and ultimately dissolved our relationship after the six months. RAM was simply thinking too small to fit into our plans. Meanwhile, though, RAM paid some of the cost of installing RightCAD at Clemente to Pinpoint.

The other important event that happened at Clemente was that we met Jennifer Jones. Jennifer was manager of Clemente's billing department. She and I spent a lot of time talking about billing programs. David, Bob, and I had always thought that we would eventually develop a billing product, but Jennifer was able to allow us to understand the amount of work that would be involved.

Out of our meetings at Clemente, we eventually brought Jennifer and two other billing managers from other companies out to Boulder for a brainstorming session on what Pinpoint's billing product might look like. In hindsight, the brainstorming session was a disaster, because the only ideas we got were about features missing from those managers' respective systems.

However, that didn't stop us and we decided to develop a billing system and use Clemente as our beta site. Jennifer would be instrumental in getting the system up and running.

Eventually we hired Jennifer, first as our receptionist and office manager. We figured that in addition to helping us out, she'd be a great resource for billing questions. So she was really our receptionist, office manager, and product manager. Eventually we hired a dedicated receptionist and then a dedicated office manager, and Jennifer remained our billing product manager for a long time.

Our Second Boulder Office

Top 10

Reasons Why The New Office Space "Rocks"

10.   Increased elbow room per employee.

9.   More room in each department for future growth with no need to move again.

8.   93% of current employees will have natural lighting and outside views.

7.   At next years user conference, we won't have to say "Yeah, we're getting that space across the hall soon."

6.   Increased privacy, autonomy and independence for departmental operations.

5.   Visiting clients will notice an improved professional image throughout the company.

4.   One step closer to having a big red rotating pin on the roof of the building.

3.   Private conference room for client meetings, demos, etc.

2.   A firm commitment to growth, improved sales, and profit sharing.

1.   Finally, a place to put all those damn bikes.

A flyer that David made up for our employees in order to generate excitement when we doubled our space at Pearl East.

In early 1996 we hired Zebeth, John, and Andy Cutright, so Pinpoint now had seven employees. There was no longer enough shag carpeting at Vern's to accommodate all of us.

David and I began the process of looking for some professional office space. When we walked into the office at 4845 Pearl East Circle in February, we immediately fell in love. The previous tenant, a marketing agency, had loaded up the space with a lot of features. It had a great open floor plan and incredible views of the mountains. We signed up almost immediately.

The 2,000 square feet at Pearl East would be our home for the next three years. In August 1997 we took over another 2,000 square feet next door, opened up a wall, and doubled our footprint.

At a time that we were beginning to court bigger companies and wanted to bring them by our office, Vern's place was just too embarrassing to host guests like these. We paid $3,000 a month in rent, up from $800 at Vern's, so the money was a stretch. We never regretted it and we felt more like a real company than ever.

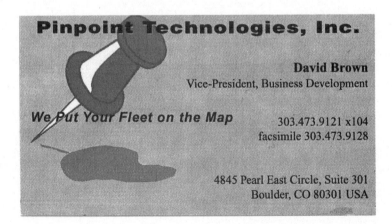

Two business cards from the Pearl East days showing what we called "the evolution of the pin."

User Conferences

Having just moved into our great new space, we held our first official user conference in March 1996. Future employees Doug Plaza and Pamela Olkowski would attend as customers. We held a portion of the conference in the empty space next door, mentioning that we would be moving into that space shortly, which wasn't true the first year. A year later, we held the second user conference in the same spot and had just signed for the same new space, so we repeated the same story, which this time was true.

At the user conferences, we made a big effort to make sure that in addition to learning a lot, our customers had fun. We would take them out at night and on the Saturday after the conference, we took anyone skiing who was interested. Early on we started the tradition of having the "Future Session," initially hosted by David, in which we would get customers excited about what we were working on or thinking about, as well as new trends in computing.

Future Sessions would always be one of the most interesting and popular sessions at our conference.

The popularity of the skiing outing led us to move the conference to Vail for the third, fourth, and fifth conferences, which we now appropriately called the Summit. In 2001, we moved back to Boulder before settling on the Westin in Westminster for the seventh and eighth installments.

All the customers who were at the user conferences in Vail remember Scott Munns, a singer we used to go see every night, year after year. Scott first noticed us because one of our attendees, a WesTech salesman named Scott Stevens, was dropping shots out of his bottom into a beer on the floor. Scott brought him up onstage and all of Vail knew our Scott as the "ass man" for the rest of the week. We started a tradition of bringing all our customers to Scott's show every night, although the ass man never made another appearance.

By the end of my tenure at Pinpoint, the planning for the Summit User Conference had become a yearlong event, with significant involvement from half a dozen employees. Through the years we retained the tradition of working hard and playing hard and tried to have the event keep us close to our customers.

Although the Summit was an expensive undertaking, costing us about $80,000 in 2003 because we didn't charge the customers an attendance fee, I feel that it was one of Pinpoint's greatest accomplishments. In addition to the valuable material that was taught, it allowed customers and employees to get to know each other and understand each other's needs better. I think that more than anything, the Summit allowed us to retain some of the family feel of the early days, even with hundreds of employees and customers.

Core Beliefs

By the end of 1998, we had 20 employees. In addition to David, Bob, Eran, and me, there were Zebeth, John, and Andy, as well as Devon McClain (David and Bob's college roommate) and Doug Plaza (hired away from a customer, MONOC). Also onboard were Al Thompson (known as Weird Al the Tattooed Freak), Ivan Sandoval, and Casey Parsons in the support department; Jason Brock and Rajiv Sankranti in R&D; Christine Daspit and Marcie Cary in administration; and longtime Pinpoint marketing employee, Dennis Burney, along with a few others.

Around this time, David spearheaded an effort to put into words what we were all about. The following is the document to which everyone in the company contributed. I think that it does a great job of describing what was important to us, at least at the time.

In summary, our core beliefs said that excellence in product and service were the most important things, followed by a good working environment for our employees. Growth and diversification was the third item mentioned, although we specifically said that they were not a goal, but rather confirmation that our first two goals had been achieved. Profitability was never mentioned.

I believe that this approach, probably the exact opposite of how many companies are usually run, was a huge contributor to our success. We were successful specifically because we didn't think about success all the time. We let it happen to us.

We, Pinpoint Technologies, exist primarily to bring truly useful and valuable software and services to our customers. Nothing shall stand in the way of this goal.

Our products and services must breed customer loyalty, and our customers must believe they have received a valuable product for a fair price. We must solve real-world problems and be a critical part of the success of our customers' business. Our customers must feel that our products and services help make their businesses substantially better.

Each day, we must strive to improve both our products and our services. We must encourage and expect each other to contribute to this process.

We are a company that prides itself on honesty and integrity. We deal fairly and ethically with customers, employees, and vendors. We never pretend to be something that we are not, or that we can deliver something that we cannot. Our promises are kept. We take responsibility for our mistakes and attempt to quickly correct them to the satisfaction of those we deal with.

Pinpoint Technologies also exists to provide a team atmosphere for its employees, where personal and professional growth is fostered, and where every day is fun and exciting.

Pinpoint is committed to employing only the best and most capable people who have the ambition to become even better. The quality of our people is a tremendous competitive advantage.

Each employee must be trusted and granted the power to do what they believe is right every day. This is a tremendous responsibility that each employee must be prepared to accept. The company will always stand behind its employees' beliefs even when they make mistakes. By doing this, we hope to promote decision-making and eliminate ignorance.

We must encourage, support, and critique each other in an open and frank manner. There is an expectation that each person will speak their mind, just as there is an expectation that each person will be open to the ideas of others.

Each employee is expected to strive to have a deep understanding of our business and our market. To this end, Pinpoint is committed to investing heavily in the training of its employees. We expect each employee to set challenging goals for themselves, and for the company. Thus, career growth will not only be possible, but shall be encouraged.

We also exist to accept the challenges and responsibilities of growth and diversification.

We must always welcome growth, as long as it does not compromise our core beliefs. Growth is not a goal, but is a confirmation of our beliefs and provides proof that we are on the right track.

We will be proud but never satisfied with our accomplishments. We shall know that we can always do better.

All facets of our company must work in unison with our core beliefs. These beliefs, along with daily progress toward fulfilling our vision, will enable us to succeed.

Pinpoint Technologies has very specific ideas about how to do business, which translates into all of its daily activities. These ideals must not be compromised. Each member of this team must also believe these things, or the company will not continue to be successful.

Chapter 5 Growing Up

Pinpoint on a Roll

Beginning in the last quarter of 1995 and through 1996, Pinpoint was on a roll. Sales in 1994 had been about $60,000, consisting almost exclusively of EMTrack support. In 1995 sales grew to about $250,000 and in 1996 sales quadrupled to almost $1 million. In addition to this growth we had a profit each year, something we have always been extremely proud of.

We instituted a profit-sharing program for our employees to encourage everyone to make decisions that were beneficial to the company. We felt that sharing our profits with our team would keep everyone moving in the same direction. That profit-sharing program is still in place today.

Our financial focus in those years was always on cash. Although I did all the bookkeeping, David was always interested in one number: how many months can we survive on no sales? I kept a spreadsheet in which I kept track of this number and we felt more comfortable as it crept up, although it's probably more accurate to say that we felt less uncomfortable about succeeding in the long term.

Sweet Computer Services

Back in 1996 it became clear that because we were former users of similar systems, we understood very clearly what needed to be implemented in our CAD system—but that when it came to billing, we were fumbling around, trying to figure out what the software should do. Whereas the challenge with RightCAD was learning how to program a Windows application, the challenge with billing was figuring out what the user wanted.

At a trade show in early 1997, I met Brad Brody, the president of Sweet Computer Services. Sweet had been founded 17 years earlier by David Sweet and had developed the biggest install base of billing systems in the EMS market. They had about 1,700 customers, most of them very small. David Sweet wanted to retire and had recently sold half of the company to Brad.

Since Brad was new to the business, he had no pride of ownership and recognized that his company was weak in a few areas. Their DOS product needed to be updated to Windows and Brad recognized that he didn't have the talent within his organization to easily make that conversion. Also, there was a great opportunity to sell CAD systems as well as billing systems. Most of Sweet's customers could have used one.

Similarly, we recognized that Sweet was strong in a number of areas that we were not. We were very worried about having to figure out how to print up billing forms and develop electronic submission formats for each state. It was clear to us that several would be required for each state and Sweet had already done this. We were also impressed with the sophisticated infrastructure that Sweet had developed to install and support their products. At that time, Pinpoint's support department was John and a couple of other guys, whereas

Sweet had a whole department, complete with tracking software and call-back mechanisms. Finally, we viewed ourselves as a very small company compared to Sweet. At the time, Sweet had about 50 employees and was doing about $3 million in annual sales, whereas Pinpoint had about 10 employees and was doing about $1 million in sales.

Brad and I quickly came up with a relationship in which Sweet would do all the sales, marketing, installation, and support of a new Windows billing product that we would call AcClaim! The deal we struck in mid-1997 was structured as follows:

- For all sales that Sweet made, they would receive 60 percent of revenues from the billing product and 40 percent of revenues from the CAD product. The percentage was lower for the CAD product because Sweet had not participated in its development.
- Pinpoint did not want or expect to be making sales, but in the event that we did make a sale we were to receive 60 percent of revenues from the billing product and 100 percent of revenues from the CAD product. Our reasoning in having a clause allowing Pinpoint to sell was that if Sweet wasn't successful in making sales, we would have no revenue and would go out of business.
- Each company would be responsible for supporting the customer to which it had sold.
- Pinpoint and Sweet would jointly develop AcClaim! Sweet was to provide the billing expertise and all the state forms, and Pinpoint was to provide the Windows programming for the core system.

Our view was that Pinpoint would be the development arm creating the product, for which we would receive 40 percent of billing sales and 60 percent of CAD sales. It's funny to think of how we viewed ourselves at the time, because the relationship didn't work out and Pinpoint ultimately had to invest in hiring a lot of people to do the state forms and in building out a support and deployment infrastructure. In doing so, Pinpoint wound up being a much larger company than Sweet, which remained at about 50 employees.

This is not to say that it was obvious that the outcome was good. Our goal at the time was to stay small and profitable. We thought that we might have more fun and fewer headaches if we just did development. Had the relationship worked out, it certainly would have resulted in Pinpoint being a different company, and in some ways a simpler and more enjoyable one.

Ultimately, the relationship with Sweet didn't work primarily because of a difference in philosophy between the two companies. We were the young whippersnappers from Colorado: brash, confident, and willing to make mistakes and fix them later. Sweet was an established company in a small town in Iowa and I believe they felt that we didn't give them enough credit for their extensive experience.

Regardless of the reason, the relationship never got off the ground, basically for two reasons: the state forms, which were the only part of the system that Sweet was responsible for developing, never seemed to work. Furthermore, Sweet didn't meet our agreed-upon sales targets.

We had a number of meetings and conversations with various members of Sweet's management team explaining how we felt. They made us a lot of promises but the situation never seemed to improve. I remember sitting down with David Sweet at a restaurant near Boulder, giving him the "this is your last chance" speech. We really wanted them to resolve their issues, but if they didn't, we were ready for a painful separation. The last straw came when they fired

Larry Castor, the only Sweet sales rep who had sold our products. We promptly hired Larry.

We had been smart enough to have a contract with Sweet that envisioned most scenarios. Because our survival depended on Sweet's success at selling not only the new billing product but also our CAD product, we put in performance clauses that allowed us to sever our ties if these minimum sales levels weren't met. This was the case, so it was pretty clear that we could part ways. What wasn't so clear was whether we'd have to pay them 40 percent of ongoing billing sales for life.

A very cordial relationship turned ugly very quickly. At the end of 1998, after an 18-month relationship, we had our new attorney, Rob Planchard, send them a letter advising them that we considered them to be in breach of contract for not delivering the state forms. Consequently, we didn't feel obligated to pay them the 40 percent.

They went nuts. They threatened countersuits and lots of legal action that could tie us up for ages and cause confusion for potential customers. We eventually settled by agreeing to give them a copy of the AcClaim! source code and let them go their own way with the product.

As part of the settlement, we agreed to take over the support of the 20 or so customers to whom Sweet had sold RightCAD. Sweet wisely understood that they could not provide adequate support to these customers without our giving Sweet access to the product. It was difficult and time consuming to take over the support of these customers, as Sweet's setup often had to be redone, sometimes almost from scratch.

Also as part of the settlement, we both agreed to change the name of the product. We chose to rename the product Sanitas and they chose to rename it WinClaim. We gambled that because they had not written the code for AcClaim! and were not familiar with Windows or our source code, they would have a nearly impossible time improving the product, while our version would continue to move forward. Our gamble paid off, as they spent two years trying to sell and improve WinClaim before scrapping it and starting all over on a new product called Amazon.

One of the big lessons I learned from the Sweet experience was the importance of settling potential lawsuits. We were under no obligation to give them a copy of the source code and really couldn't justify doing so. However, years of litigation might have caused potential customers to delay purchases. It was better to give up a little something that we didn't need to in order to close the chapter and move on.

We spent the next two years improving our billing product, often changing around concepts that Sweet had told us were immutable. David and I often debated whether the product would have been better or worse without Sweet's initial involvement. Although David felt that we wasted a lot of time redoing concepts that we knew weren't right in the first place, I remain convinced that because we didn't have the billing background that Sweet did, we might never have created a product that successfully served the needs of our customers.

In the end, the relationship with Sweet lasted about two years and completely transformed Pinpoint. Perhaps the relationship was doomed from the start, as our corporate cultures, experiences, and geographic locations were so different. For all the headaches, though, I still feel that the experience was a positive one. We ended up with a great billing product and we were forced to grow up as a company.

TransCare

After Clemente, our next big sale was to TransCare in New York. TransCare would be our second billing install, and it was a huge undertaking due to their large size.

Since my departure, TransCare had developed a plan to consolidate all the remote dispatch centers. They were moving them into very nice facilities they had recently acquired in Queens. They needed to decide what dispatch and what billing systems they would use in the new facilities.

I got a call from my old friend Sean Cunningham, the CFO at TransCare. In typical Sean fashion, he blurted out what was on his mind: "Your dispatch system is great, but what we really need is a billing system." Luckily, I was able to respond that we were working on it. While we had not yet become involved with Sweet, we had just had Jennifer Jones and the two other billing managers attend our disastrous planning meeting. After Sean and some other folks from TransCare took a few brief trips to Boulder, David and I went to New York to do a demo for all interested parties, including TransCare's new CEO, Ian Spira, and their bankers.

One of the folks appointed to help evaluate the system was Pamela Olkowski, TransCare's newly hired director of reimbursement. Many years later, Pamela would become a full-time Pinpoint employee living in Boulder.

Sean made it clear to us that he wanted a billing system more than he wanted a dispatch system. We told him that we were well under way in developing one and showed him some of our screen mock-ups. Clearly Sean believed in us, because he accepted this bald-faced exaggeration at face value. Pamela recalls that she got the impression that Sean, her boss at the time, had already made up his mind. For her part, she saw absolutely nothing in the software that would work for her operation.

Most of the next year was consumed in getting TransCare up and running. TransCare was a huge operation, running 300 ambulances and wheelchair vans and doing 2,500 calls a day. Our software had not yet been optimized to dispatch that many calls, much less bill for them.

I traveled to TransCare almost every month. We dialed in and tried to diagnose problems day and night. David, John Stapleton, and I did most of the direct support work, but the process involved the whole company.

An example will give you an idea of the severity of some of the problems. One problem was that sometimes the system would lock up and then nobody could use their terminals. The only way to clear the problem was to dial in and clear a lock on the server. Because it was a dispatch operation downtime could quickly become very critical, so at times we had someone dialed in and watching the system from 6 a.m. to 6 p.m. (the peak time for lockups). That was the only way to keep the system going.

John Stapleton spent most of Christmas and New Year's of 1997 in the TransCare office trying to diagnose a single problem. John had traveled back to New York to visit his family for the holidays, but the problem was so severe that he had to get a hotel room near TransCare's office and work.

Eventually we worked through all the issues in both dispatch and billing. Throughout the whole process, we were very lucky to have Pamela overseeing the billing implementation, as a less patient person would have kicked us out early on. Also of immeasurable assistance was TransCare's incredibly bright, if a bit nerdy, director of IT, Kirk Amico.

Ultimately, all the work would pay off many times over, as TransCare gave us several keys to success:

- The brutal process of eliminating all the bugs and making the software run quickly and efficiently in a large operation allowed us to have a solid, efficient software application.

- We had a reference site for potential customers who might be concerned that the software wouldn't work for them. TransCare was such a large, diverse, and complex organization that everyone who saw the system or spoke to them realized that our software had to be very flexible. For a while it seemed that we brought every single potential client to TransCare's offices to see the system in action. Almost every one of the customers that we brought to TransCare ultimately purchased our system.
- We learned an enormous amount about billing through the implementation, thanks again largely to Pamela's input. This knowledge allowed us to realize that we should sever our relationship with Sweet and create an even stronger billing product.
- We sold TransCare the entire system for less than $200,000, quite a bargain by Pinpoint's current pricing standards, but some of those progress payments, although notoriously late, kept us from going bankrupt.

Looking back, that one sale to TransCare was a key to the ultimate success of Pinpoint. It was enormously hard work, but it gave our product the stability and our company the credibility it needed to get going.

Unfortunately, TransCare took a bad turn shortly after the system was up and running. They merged with another New York–based company of the same size and were ultimately taken over by the CEO of that company, Steve Zacheim. Although we tried to get Steve interested in our CAD and billing systems, he ultimately was against anything TransCare had endorsed and stuck with his in-house systems. Fortunately, this all occurred after we had gotten the momentum we needed out of TransCare. Their demise as our premier reference client didn't hurt all that much.

Going International

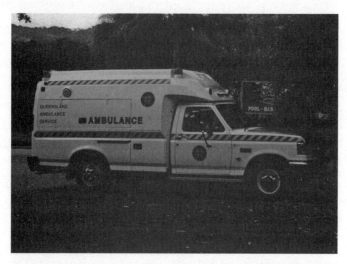

An ambulance in Australia (note that in typical Pinpoint fashion, this picture was taken in front of a bar).

A picture of RightCAD running in the Queensland dispatch center.

In 1997 we were approached by a company called SCC to help them out with an ambulance client in Australia. SCC, which coincidentally was located in Boulder, sold dispatch systems for police, fire, and EMS. Because we specialized in EMS, we did not consider them a competitor.

SCC's Australian customer, Queensland Ambulance Service (QAS), had a need for functionality that SCC didn't provide. This functionality—scheduling prearranged, non-emergency ambulance rides—was a feature of our products.

SCC, who later sold the rights to their product to Printrak, who then sold the company to Motorola, was faced with the need to either develop this extra functionality or to contract with a company whose product already had it. They did a Web search and found us just down the road. Bob and I drove up and were extremely impressed with their operation. They were in a big building, had "Welcome Pinpoint" displayed on monitors, and just seemed like a huge company. We laughed, though, about their referring to their installation process as a "deployment," since it made the process seem so complex. Later, as we grew and our installations became more complex, we adopted their terminology.

> One of the most impressive things about SCC was their conference room. Anyone who was in their building will tell you about it. One wall of the conference room was opaque glass. They sat you down at a table and told you about their "network operations center." The product was providing 911 caller ID for phone companies around the country, and when they finished telling their story, they pressed a button and the opaque glass wall suddenly became transparent, showing the center on the other side. On the far wall was a huge electronic map of the United States, with red dots appearing as 911 calls came in. The

center was probably just for show, but it was even staffed by a few people, pushing buttons and changing the displays. I was later told that a bell rang when the button was pressed and the glass turned transparent, so that the staffers would know when they were "on."

The outcome of that and subsequent meetings was that SCC became our distributor in Australia, selling their first and, as it turns out, only system to QAS. To help convince QAS that this was in their best interests, I traveled to Australia to do a demo to a number of their people. One of their assistant commissioners, Jim Higgins, took the lead on the project and traveled to New York to visit TransCare with me.

By April 1997 John Stapleton and then David traveled to Australia to help with the deployment process, and the customer went live with great success.

QAS is arguably the largest ambulance company in the world and having them as a customer certainly helped our message that our system was world class. Although the distributorship with SCC, and subsequently Printrak, never worked out as we had hoped, having QAS as an early international customer taught us a lot about the process of internationalizing our product, such as international date formats, different formats for phone numbers, and metric measurements. In addition, supporting and selling systems from a long distance away gave us a lot of credibility.

Working with a Distributor

Although we were very happy to have QAS as a customer and were appropriately paid for the deal, we expected SCC to sell more systems in Australia. We expressed our concerns to SCC to no avail. When SCC sold the rights to Printrak, we felt we had a new opportunity and made a pitch to David Leggett, the head of Printrak in Australia. David seemed like he would breathe new life into the distributorship, but nothing happened. Finally, things only got worse when Printrak was acquired by Motorola, a company far too big to be interested in tiny old Pinpoint.

It would be a good lesson for me in the pitfalls of having a distributor. The advantage was that we had an opportunity to sell in a faraway place without having to hire staff and figure out local laws, taxes, and customs. The disadvantage was that we had very little control over the distributor, as we weren't his only source of revenue and he put his efforts where he thought he could get the most bang for the buck. That clearly wasn't with us.

Eventually, in 2001, ZOLL would face similar issues with their distributor in Australia and open a direct operation, hiring their own staff and working through the issues. We were able to piggyback on this effort and hire our own sales and support folks and terminate our agreement with Motorola/Printrak. We were subsequently no more successful in Australia than our distributor was.

Chapter 6 A Personal Milestone

In April 1998 my friend Nancy Boyd invited me on what's referred to in Colorado as a "hut trip." The hut we went to was called Francie's Cabin, and it was located in the middle of the wilderness, up at the edge of the tree line, at around 10,500 feet. Francie's, like many other huts in the Colorado 10th Mountain Division hut system, sleeps more than 20 people and is fully stocked with beds, pots, pans, utensils, and board games. There is solar-powered electricity, a sauna, and other comforts that belie the remoteness. Friends of Nancy's had rented out the entire hut for a long weekend and we set out early on a Saturday morning with a large group. We snowshoed uphill for hours, with two days of gear and rations on our backs.

One of the other hikers, also a last-minute add-in, was Kris Hiemstra, whom I would marry less than two years later. Kris and I didn't talk that much on the trip, but we did get together a few weeks later for another hike in the Boulder area.

Kris and I seemed destined to be together from the start. Before either of us realized what was happening, we were going on vacations together, meeting each other's families, and spending all of our time together. We got engaged in July of 1999 and got married on the eve of the millennium, December 31, 1999.

Kris has always been a great support in my efforts to grow Pinpoint. She was present on the day I met the CEO of ZOLL and was supportive during all the long hours of the process of selling to ZOLL. Life was evolving quickly and she took all the changes in stride, never letting them affect her negatively.

She has been a great partner all along.

Chapter 7 Growing the Company

After TransCare we were off to the races. We grew steadily and faced a steady stream of new operational problems. We referred to the sales process as "both feet on the brakes," because if we sold too much we weren't able to install and support the new customers. We felt strongly that customer satisfaction was too important to give up.

Our growth was pretty steady over the years, both in terms of the number of employees and the amount of sales. By 1999 we were riding pretty high. We had finally penetrated Rural/Metro, the second-largest ambulance company in the United States, and they were purchasing several systems for their operations nationwide. Meanwhile, the Y2K scare was causing customers that had older CAD systems to want to upgrade. We played up the fact that our system was conceived and written for Windows and had always been Y2K compliant. That certainly helped our sales.

One of the painful lessons we learned early on was that management by consensus doesn't work. In the early days whenever there was an important decision to be made, we'd gather everyone around and talk it out. As we grew, it became impossible to get everyone to agree on any one decision. Then invariably, when we'd decide on something, those who had taken the opposing view felt that they weren't being listened to. This drove the need to set up a good structure with separate groups having responsibility and accountability for decisions.

We felt great that we were able to run a successful company that was an enjoyable place to work while maintaining our integrity. We never had to cheat or lie our way to success, we tried to do the right thing by customers, employees, vendors, and ourselves, and it always paid off. One of the things that helped is that we put great effort into creating a good corporate structure, with different departments handling different tasks and a person or group in charge of every detail of running the business. This created accountability, but more importantly, responsibility. Visitors would often comment on how surprised or impressed they were with all the structure. This was something I never tired of hearing.

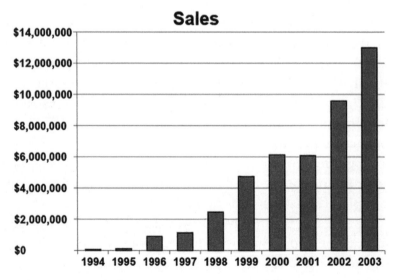

Growth in sales . . .

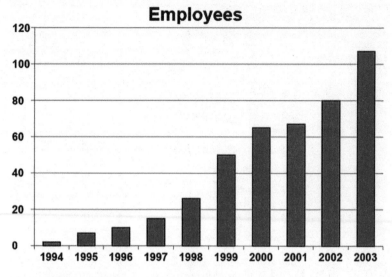

Employees

... **and in number of employees**

Buying a Building

In early 1999 we were ready to move out of our second Boulder office and became interested in buying a building. We wanted to have a fixed cost, as rents at that time seemed to be going up fast and the mortgage payment would be about the same amount as rent but would never increase. We also viewed a real estate purchase as a diversification. Things were getting big and out of control at Pinpoint. We figured if the whole company fell apart at least we would own some real estate.

We found a two-story building that was perfectly suited for us. We could move into the upstairs portion right away. A company called Green Mountain Geophysics rented the downstairs and we could move into their space when we grew enough to need it.

We were so excited that we probably struck a deal too quickly. We didn't negotiate enough on price and as it turned out, the tenant had a right to renew their lease for three years. We knew this before we signed on the dotted line, but

Special Supplemental Field
Edition to the Funion.

Pinpoint Office 2000

Boulder,
CO

January 20, 1999

After days of interviews with the staff of Pinpoint Technologies, the reporters who contributed to this special edition all felt a sense of learning the true nature of one of the worlds most dynamic companies. Traded on HUTDAQ under the ticker symbol "LITOM" (legends in their own minds), this company is literally going places. They will relocate from their current digs to the sprawling splendor of "the 1800 building" this April. Read on and be amazed.

Sneaking around New Building "really cool"

By Shirley U. Gest
AARP staff reporter

On site at 1800 38th Street

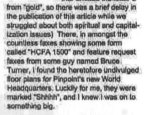

Random buildings, not ours.

After several minutes of investigative reporting, and having had my new jacket ripped nearly to shreds catching it on the corner of the dumpster in the parking lot at 4845 Pearl East Circle, I had finally found gold. (*Ed. Note:* Originally, the author omitted the letter L from "gold", so there was a brief delay in the publication of this article while we struggled about both spiritual and capitalization issues) There, in amongst the countless faxes showing some form called "HCFA 1500" and feature request faxes from some guy named Bruce Turner, I found the heretofore undivulged floor plans for Pinpoint's new World Headquarters. Luckily for me, they were marked "Shhhh", and I knew I was on to something big.

Wasting no time, I gathered my over-the-counter counter-surveillance gear and set out that very night to check things out. Upon entering the building, I soon realized that the new office space Pinpoint Technologies was moving into was

actually really cool. After turning the A/C down, I thought I'd dig deeper into the innate coolness factor that obviously existed inside the walls of Pinpoint's new World Headquarters.

I proceeded up the main stairwell under the cover of darkness into what will soon become Pinpoint's new digs. Luckily my many years of training at the ITPT (Institute for the Training of Professional Thieves) allowed me to easily defeat the surprisingly sophisticated alarm systems that were in place upstairs. I referred to my hard-earned floor plan (see page 3) and realized I had found the reception area. It would be here that Marcie Cary would fend off the capitalistic vultures that try to prey on young, successful software companies, and who seem to empty the candy bowl in the process.

I decided to walk straight ahead and found the President's office, a demonstration room, and a sizeable conference room behind nice glass. I chuckled as I thought to myself, "Yeah, that Brown character deserves to be in a fishbowl." At the end of the hallway, I found Bob Durkin's office. I envisioned his head being the only visible part of his body behind his desk.

Making a left, I encountered what appeared to be a small hockey rink. Upon closer inspection, I found an enormous kitchen and employee lounge. I checked, and there was no food. I made a note to visit Taco Bell, because I was hungry.

Continuing down the hallway to the northern side of the building, I found what had been labeled on the floor plan as the

(Continued on page 2)

1

> "This March, Pinpoint moves into its new building, which is four times the size of its current space."

Sneaking around was "Really Cool"

(Continued from page 1)

"Deployment" department, I thought to myself, "deployment", gee, what a big word. I realized it must be a sizable department within the company because it had three large offices assigned to it. Then I thought, maybe those people have big long titles too, so they need more space.

The fourth office down the hall was the corporate operations office. Actually, whoever had drawn the floor plan had crossed that off, and put the word "Office Manager," I guess they had envisioned bigger things to come. Just outside this office was the supply area, where one would put fax machines, "pasta schmeras", copiers, and other useless beeping devices. It would be here that the famous "kanban" system for office supplies would be mocked well into the future.

The fifth office down the large hall was marked "MIS." From here, Kevin Slusher would rule his empire of phones, wiring, and servers. The keypad on the door would ensure the staff could keep Kevin where he could do the least harm.

Just past the MIS office was what appeared to me to be an escape stairwell. I realized the brilliance in this as I thought about how easy support staffers could duck out when Marci gave the signal that clients were near. It provided easy access to a waiting getaway car.

We next came to the Technical Support area. Here, many people wearing funny headsets would interact with lucky callers, and console them about their houses burning down, or worse yet, that damn GPF when adding a payor in call taking. I thought I heard a ghost say "Do you have the latest service pack?", but I must have

imagined it.

Behind the technical support area, the floor plan called for a Sales and Marketing area. I could almost see Larry's empty docking station, and Dennis yelling "damn it" at PhotoShop.

In the southwestern corner of the building, I found what was succinctly labeled "R&D", Research and Destroy, would be my guess. In this area would also be the new Quality Assurance Lab and the Product Management Office.

I then went downstairs, where Green Mountain Geophysics (www.gmg.com) rents out the bottom floor from Pinpoint. These guys create software for the petroleum industry. You know "Black Gold, Texas Tea". I was able to jimmy the lock to Green Mountain pretty easily, and I saw a veritable plethora (that's more than 20 in reporter lingo) of private offices downstairs, plus several nice meeting areas. I thought I heard a right-click in one of the offices downstairs, so I introduced myself as the new janitorial administrator to some longhaired guy working late. He seemed like a nice enough person, immediately offering me his garbage. But I know how those software companies can be.

"Damn", I thought to myself, "it's still cool in here."

Pinpoint at a Glance

Employees:	28
Telephone lines:	21
Computers:	33
Morons:	3
Modems:	24
LAN GB online:	70
Clients:	78
Annual Sales:	2.9M
BBQ Grills:	1
Programmers:	7
Support Techs:	7
Blazing Typists:	1
Countries Dominated:	3
Data source: 1999 Big Business Book of Non-Sensus	

2

A brochure that David Cohen put together to pump up excitement about the new building. We had 28 employees, 21 telephone lines, 33 computers, 24 modems, 70GB of LAN space in use, 78 clients, and $2.9 million in annual sales.

we were under the impression from the seller that the tenant didn't intend to renew, but they did.

Fortunately, things worked out. The tenant thought that because the building had a new owner we could kick them out. We didn't correct them on this error and six months later we took over their space downstairs.

The building was technically owned by a different company, Pinpoint Property Management, which was owned by David, Bob, and me. This gave us some extra protection, so if someone sued Pinpoint Technologies, our investment in the building would be protected.

> When we moved into the building our vision was to set up an environment similar to the Miami dispatch center's. We invited a local client, Pridemark Paramedics, to set up their Boulder dispatch office in what became our conference room. We figured they could put staff in there and we could use the site to show customers and employees our software in action. Pridemark was growing, though, and was soon going to need a bigger space than our conference room allowed, so the arrangement ultimately didn't work out.

Integrated Management Solutions

As if we didn't have enough irons in the fire, in April 1999 we helped start up our third company, Integrated Management Solutions, with Pamela Olkowski. Pinpoint Technologies was our main focus, with Pinpoint Property Management being our foray into the real estate business. IMS was really a way to hire Pamela Olkowski without letting the outside world know she was part of Pinpoint.

In our years of working with various billing operations, we had seen how companies struggled to run their operations efficiently. When we'd worked with her at TransCare, Pamela had seemed to understand the complexities of those systems far better than anyone we had ever met.

David, Bob, and I saw a need to provide our customers with consulting services for their billing operations, but we were concerned that if we provided this service as part of the software sale, customers would be confused about what they were buying from Pinpoint. We had always maintained the position that they were buying software, and that how they used it was up to them.

David, Bob, and I took a 50 percent stake in IMS and Pamela took the other half. When we sold Pinpoint to ZOLL a few months later we were concerned that they might consider our ownership stake in IMS a conflict of interest, so we turned over our shares to Pamela.

Pamela ran the company out of the Pinpoint offices in Boulder for a few years. Although she was very successful in providing consulting services, she struggled to sell and market those services. In 2002 she left to take a regular job in Denver. Her services were so sorely missed, however, that we hired her back as an employee a year later, in May 2003. We decided that the overhead of her running IMS wasn't worth it. Customers were able to distinguish between her services and our software.

Exit Strategies

It was in this high-growth environment that we started to think of an exit strategy. Up to this point we had never had one. We just figured we'd have fun and see where the company took us, never once thinking about what would be next.

Sometime in 1997, though, we started to realize that we might want to get investors or sell the company some day. Why? Certainly the idea of getting some financial security in return for our hard work played a part. A bigger reason, though, was the enormous responsibility that Pinpoint was becoming. With more and more employees, all of whom depended on us to keep providing a paycheck, the days of skipping a paycheck to make payroll for everyone else were long gone. Other than a $35,000 line of credit with the bank, we had no financial resources to draw on and now burned through a lot more than that every month. Should sales slow down even for a short period of time, we would undoubtedly miss payroll and go out of business. We had a strong sense of our own mortality, with exploding sales leading to a rapidly growing number of employees, which resulted in substantial expenses. And we had no safety net.

The thought had crossed our minds that TransCare might buy us someday. Had they been successful in consolidating ambulance companies nationwide, it certainly would have made sense for them to lock up the software by buying us so they would have control of feature development and would be able to prevent competitors from having access to our software. This scenario, however, never developed beyond just a thought.

We were also approached by a couple of venture capitalists, including the one that had funded ADS (Philadelphia Venture Partners) and the one that had funded TransCare (Morgan Stanley). Both wanted to wait until we were a bit larger before doing anything and so nothing happened. That was probably just as well, as we had a bad impression of VCs from our ADS days. If you get into trouble VCs can bail you out and give you more money, but you pay a hefty price, giving up a good chunk of the company's stock and control in the process.

We were approached by a potential suitor in early 1998. The company, Constellation Software, owned Trapeze, another software company that sold computer-aided dispatch systems to the paratransit market. While Constellation Software wasn't a competitor because they sold to another market, they were interested in getting into EMS so had sought us out as a potential acquisition target.

At that time we really had no intention of selling, but their interest led us to think that we might sell someday. We decided to go through the process and see how it worked. We figured that the worst thing that could happen is that we would learn a lot about acquisitions and that it was possible they would make us an offer that we couldn't refuse.

The process was very interesting. Constellation sent down one individual, who looked through our books and spent a whole day asking a lot of good questions. In the end they made us a proposal that wasn't too bad, but that was less than we felt the company was worth. The biggest problem with the deal was that 50 percent of the number they gave us wasn't real. It was a 50 percent cash deal, with the other 50 percent being an investment in a company that we would jointly own (with 51 percent of the control going to Constellation). This was really a bet on the future, rather than a payment for the company. Of course, it made sense that this is what they would want, as it would motivate us to make sure the new company was successful. In the end, we said no thanks and never heard from them again. Constellation's subsidiary, Trapeze, tried to modify their product and sell it to the EMS market, but they were never successful and eventually withdrew.

Chapter 8 The Sale to ZOLL

The sale of Pinpoint to ZOLL Medical started in much the same way as the experience with Constellation: it began as a practice exercise in negotiating an acquisition. What changed is that they made us an offer we couldn't refuse.

I'd met Rick Packer, the president of ZOLL, by sheer coincidence: I sat next to him at a lunch at a user conference being held by WesTech Mobile Solutions in Vancouver, Canada, in August 1998. I believe that this chance encounter set things in motion and ultimately led to the sale of Pinpoint to ZOLL.

WesTech Mobile Solutions was based in Vancouver and had developed a product that complemented our dispatch and billing products. Their software product, EMS Pro, charted events that occurred in the ambulance, such as the administration of drugs and the taking of vital signs. Their product ran on a tablet-style computer that was portable and supported handwriting recognition.

ZOLL, based in a suburb of Boston, Massachusetts, was the world's second largest manufacturer of defibrillators—devices that restart the heart after a person goes into cardiac arrest. Defibrillators and the WesTech system capture a lot of the same information, so ZOLL had purchased WesTech in 1996.

Pinpoint had an informal relationship with WesTech. Keith Lyon, the general manager of WesTech, had sought us out to see if we could do some joint marketing activities. As the relationship grew, Keith introduced me to some of the higher-ups in the ZOLL organization, generally VPs or directors. Keith was pushing for a more formal relationship between ZOLL/WesTech and Pinpoint. At that time, I was extremely underwhelmed by the ZOLL corporate types I met. They seemed stiff and uninterested in understanding why we could do more together than apart. This was fine by me because we were benefiting more from the informal relationship than they were. They had introduced us to a number of their large customers, such as Hall Ambulance, Medix Ambulance, and MEMS, to whom we'd sold our CAD and/or billing products. None of the customers we introduced WesTech to ultimately purchased their product.

In the course of visiting these mutual customers we came to realize that WesTech had a lot of problems. The ZOLL sales force sold their product, and product support was handled in Boston by the ZOLL service department, which reported to ZOLL's VP of operations. Meanwhile, programming and deployment were done from the Vancouver office, which reported through Keith to Rick, the president of ZOLL. All these different reporting structures caused a lot of finger-pointing. Keith felt that the support in Boston was ineffective and was lobbying ZOLL to move it to Vancouver. The R&D department was scrambling to create features that the sales department in Boston said they needed in order to sell the product—or worse yet, to support systems they had already sold. So much time was being spent creating these vaporware features that not enough effort was being put into stabilizing the product and making it bug free. The result was that sales were virtually nonexistent and WesTech was losing over $1 million per year.

So when I sat down to lunch and realized that I was sitting next to the president of ZOLL, I already had two impressions of the company: that two of the higher-ups I had met were a couple of stooges, and that the company had set up a structure that was causing nothing but problems. I figured I would ask Rick why he had organized things this way. I was completely blown away by Rick. I was expecting a third stooge, but Rick was well aware of all of WesTech's problems and attempted to put everything in a bigger context. Despite his efforts he didn't convince me that things at WesTech were all roses, but all I could say after his responses was "Okay, it's your company, you know best." Rick had brought his wife, Cori, to Vancouver and Bob Durkin and I were both there with our wives as well. We wound up having a very nice lunch and we all got along very well.

My intention in asking Rick these questions was only to try to gain an understanding of why he ran his company the way he did. I never thought that I had impressed him, but I guess I did, because the next thing I knew we were "summoned" to Boston to meet some of the ZOLL team members. Keith was the intermediary who organized the trip, saying, "ZOLL wants to talk to you, can you be there on Tuesday?" So Bob Durkin and I booked flights for Tuesday.

In November 1998 Bob and I met with Rick, Rolf Stutz, then the CEO of ZOLL, and Ward Hamilton, their VP of marketing. They asked us a lot of questions, much as Constellation had. Ward led us through an exercise that I now realize was an effort to size the market, our share, and the market's overall potential. He asked questions like "Who are your major competitors?," "How many systems have they sold?," and "How many ambulance companies do you think there are in the US?"

Bob and I answered as best we could, but in many cases we had to guess and use our best judgment. Then Ward summed everything up and put it all together. Bob and I suddenly realized that there was logic behind the whole thing and that Ward was testing us to see if the sum of the parts equaled the whole. After he summarized everything, Bob and I both sighed in relief when our guesses all wound up being quite close. The meeting lasted several hours, and in the end, they basically said, "Thanks for coming." So we went home. We really had no idea what the meeting was about.

After a few days, we heard from Keith that the meeting had gone extremely well.

"Rick and Rolf never sit through long meetings," said Keith. "You must have really impressed them."

A few days later Rolf called and said that they were interested in taking the next step. He made it clear that what they were potentially interested in was outright acquisition; they weren't interested in any other deal.

"If that sounds okay," he said, "I'd like to come out to Boulder and talk to you some more."

So in December 1998 Rolf came to Boulder. He had founded ZOLL in 1984 with Dr. Paul Zoll, who had invented the pacemaker in the 1950s. He had overseen taking the company public and had shepherded the growth of the company since the beginning. In 1996 he had appointed Rick as president and had partially retired. Rolf had been diagnosed with cancer and passed away soon after the Pinpoint acquisition was complete. I heard so many great stories about him and regret not having had the opportunity to get to know him better.

In Boulder Rolf continued to ask questions and learn more about our company, our products, our ideas, and our goals. Shortly after his return to Boston, he brought his newly hired CFO, Ernie Whiton, into the process. For years David, Bob, and I had been exposed to entrepreneurs and small-company types. Rick, Rolf, and Ernie all had MBAs from Harvard, and we were extremely impressed with their ability to quickly understand issues and apply business logic to situations. It turns out that they no longer employed the stooges from ZOLL whom I had met earlier, so I guess they also knew how to cut their losses and move on. Ernie asked us for financial statements, a list of employee titles and salaries, and a few other documents.

In January 1999 we were again summoned to Boston. This time I went with David. We met with Rolf, Rick, and Ernie. Rick started the meeting by doing a presentation about ZOLL. David and I still didn't view it as likely that we would sell Pinpoint to ZOLL. Once again, we were practicing in case we did want to sell someday. We had done very little research on ZOLL, didn't know anything about their products, their competitors, or their business, and didn't really care to. We didn't see any synergy in selling to a company whose product sent electricity through people. There had seemed to be better synergy between Pinpoint and Constellation. Rick was a masterful presenter, though, and as he walked us through the business, including some of the technologies that they had recently introduced, we became more and more impressed with ZOLL. Finally, Ernie laid out an offer. It was extremely simple, presented on a single page. We were to receive shares of ZOLL stock, a four-year employment agreement at double our salaries plus the possibility of a big bonus, and some ZOLL stock options. Ernie did a great job of showing what all these items added up would be worth over a three-year period, making the number seem extremely large.

ZOLL would have preferred a more complex deal, one in which the purchase price was tied to performance. At the very least, they would have liked to create what are called golden handcuffs, whereby we would not receive the stock unless we continued working for Pinpoint for at least four years. They were very concerned that we would leave after the deal was done and felt that the value of the software would be drastically reduced if the people who had put it together were no longer with the company.

ZOLL wanted to structure the deal, however, as something called a "pooling of interests," which in legal terms meant that ZOLL wasn't buying Pinpoint but rather that the two companies were merging—even though Rick was to be my boss, which effectively meant that we were being bought. Under pooling of interests rules, golden handcuffs aren't allowed. In the end, David, Bob, and I simply made a gentlemen's agreement with Rick that we wouldn't leave.

We were very skeptical of the way Ernie had put together the numbers. For one thing, some of his assumptions were based on ZOLL's stock price going up, making the deal much more valuable. At that time the stock was trading at around $9 per share, but Ernie did his calculations using the assumption that the stock might go as high as $28 per share. Because we were being offered shares, if the stock price more than tripled, as Ernie and Rick had suggested, the value of the deal more than tripled. We viewed this arrangement as being paid in futures, just as in the Constellation deal. If we sold the company, we wanted a fixed amount now, not the possibility of lots of cash later. As owners of Pinpoint, we would always have the possibility of lots of cash later; we didn't need to sell the company to get that. The second concern was that it was an all-stock deal. Even though ZOLL was publicly traded, which meant that the stock could be sold anytime we wanted, we were concerned that somehow we might get caught if the stock went down before we converted to cash. In theory the stock could lose a lot of its value and the deal could become practically worthless.

We were no experts in this area. None of us had ever worked for a publicly traded company, held any stock options, or had any real understanding of stock value. We learned as we went and tried to figure things out while seeking out people who might be able to answer our questions, such as our lawyer, our accountant, and our personal financial planner. In a matter of weeks, we tried to learn everything we could about trading volumes, P/E ratios, and market caps.

After expressing some of these concerns to ZOLL, David and I got back on the plane and supplied our own, more conservative view of what the deal was worth. Rather than assuming that the stock was going to grow from $9 to $28, we assumed that it stayed at $9. As owners of Pinpoint, we could pay ourselves whatever we wanted to, so we stripped out the portion of ZOLL's equation that included the extra salary. In the end, we had a much smaller number. The funny thing was that that number was still big enough to be interesting. David and I looked at each other and said, "Maybe we counter with 20 percent more and then we settle on 10 percent more. Done!" That plane ride home was the first time that we suddenly realized that the sale might actually happen. We were giddy with excitement.

As soon as we got home, after filling in Bob on all the details, we decided to get ZOLL even more excited about buying Pinpoint and to make a counteroffer. We set about putting together a proposal book. It was a lot like the early days of Pinpoint, with David, Bob, and me doing all the work, including printing and binding. We tried to show that we understood why they wanted to buy us and tried to articulate a vision of what we would bring to the partnership. They had given us numbers on what they thought WesTech would be able to achieve over the next few years, so we combined that with the Pinpoint projections and added some specific assumptions about how much a joint operation could increase sales and reduce overhead, creating ever more profit for ZOLL. We made the argument that ZOLL would recoup twice what they had offered us in three years. So we asked for twice as much, half in cash and half in stock. We were happy with their proposal, but that didn't mean we couldn't negotiate.

After submitting the proposal to ZOLL, we anxiously awaited their reply. It came in the form of a phone call from Rolf, who spent a lot of time explaining the rules of a pooling of interests transaction. They would not be able to pay us 50 percent cash, he said, not because they didn't want to, but because that would blow the pooling of interests arrangement and they would have to show the entire acquisition as a loss on their books. This would be disastrous to their stock price and therefore their shareholders. They simply couldn't move on that point. We could sell the stock on the open market, but again, under a pooling of interests arrangement, that wouldn't be allowed until 90 days after the merger. Because we had asked for 50 percent in cash, we added another gentlemen's agreement that we would only sell half of the stock in the first four years. Once we had agreed to that point, Rolf said, they would consider our proposal. So we agreed.

What happened next was what we called "the big wait." Rolf called and said that they had some other deal, unrelated to us, and they had to delay us for six months. I never did find out what the other deal was, although I almost got it out of Ernie once. So we waited, not without a great deal of uneasiness.

Six months later, in July 1999, we picked up where we left off. Rick called and said that he and Ernie would like to come to Boulder to talk some more. Little did we know that after some intense discussions and negotiations, we would have a binding letter of intent signed within a week. This letter of intent outlined all the key points of the deal.

Ernie and Rick came out within a few days. It was one all-day visit, and during that day we struck a deal. We decided to start off with a show-and-tell that demonstrated our products. We emphasized a new product that we had been working on, although had not yet released, called Nomad. Nomad was a product that ran on inexpensive hardware inside the ambulance. Although it was primarily designed to be a mobile data terminal that told the driver where to go and allowed them to easily document when the vehicle had arrived on scene, we also showed how Nomad could do some field data collection. Our intent was to show them that their WesTech product might one day become obsolete in the face of a competitor that ran on much less expensive hardware. We wanted them to know that if they didn't buy us, we would likely be competitors. This had the desired effect, because later on Ernie told me that he had said to Rick during a break that day that they needed to buy us or we might put WesTech out of business.

Our negotiating position was considerably weakened by a major factor. Six months earlier when we had made our counterproposal to ZOLL, we had insisted that the deal be expressed in terms of dollars, not shares of ZOLL stock. We did this because we didn't buy into ZOLL's argument that the stock was worth more than its stock price and was bound to go up. We felt it was very volatile and might likely go down and we didn't want that to affect us negatively. Of course, ZOLL was right, and six months later when they came up with a counteroffer in dollars, the stock had risen from $9 to $15, making their original offer that much more valuable. The way it was to work was that on the day the deal was done, we were to calculate an average share price over the previous few days and determine how many shares we would get based on that average. So under their original offer valued in stock, the more the stock price went up before the deal was done, the better it was for us. Under our counteroffer valued in fixed dollars, the more the stock went up before the deal was done, the worse it was for us.

The negotiation went back and forth a couple of times with offers and counteroffers. In the end we agreed on a dollar amount. ZOLL said that they wanted to have a letter of intent signed right away and have the whole deal done in about three months, on October 15, 1999.

In the three days or so that the lawyers were fighting about the details of the letter of intent, ZOLL's stock kept going up—by a lot. This was bad for us. We would still get the dollar amount we had agreed on, but we would not reap the extra benefit from the stock price going up, as it would have already done so. When the stock hit $20 and the letter of intent still hadn't been signed, I convinced Rick to convert the deal back to number of shares right then, meaning if the stock went up more, we would benefit. It was an eleventh-hour move that put the value of the deal back somewhere close to ZOLL's original offer. So much for all the negotiations!

After the letter of intent was signed, we nervously watched the stock price. Could the $20 have been an anomaly? Would it go back down? Luckily for us, the stock kept going up: it quickly hit $24 and then gradually went up to about $26 on the day we closed the deal. By the time the waiting period was over and we could sell the stock, it was up to $37, almost doubling the value of the sale to us compared to when we had locked in the price.

The next three months leading up to the close of the deal saw a flurry of activity. ZOLL had to send out auditors to do a complete audit of our books. Because we were privately held and not under the scrutiny of anyone, we were a long way from using GAAP (generally accepted accounting principles) and had to clean everything up to conform. Because I had no accounting background (and no bookkeeper), I had to quickly learn the principles of when to recognize revenue, how to accrue for vacation time, and countless other details.

I also had to do a presentation for ZOLL's board of directors. The deal was big enough that Rick wanted to get their approval. I arrived in Boston with a few slides to show. Ernie gave me some ideas and I reworked the entire presentation at the very last minute. Fortunately, Ernie's suggestions were excellent and even though I felt completely in over my head in this environment, I was able to get through the presentation looking knowledgeable and professional. There were a few questions and then I was excused while the board discussed the deal.

Rick emerged from the meeting and let me know that the board had given conditional approval, with the condition being that we seek an amendment to our contract with AID (now Rural/Metro). The problem was that the ZOLL lawyers had found a clause in the agreement that could be interpreted as entitling Rural/Metro to a 2.5 percent royalty not only on Pinpoint sales, but also WesTech sales and perhaps even ZOLL sales. Rick said, "Just so you understand, Dave, this is a deal killer, we can't proceed without the amendment."

So a week or so later I flew to Rural/Metro headquarters in Phoenix. Fortunately, we had been selling systems to them and had a relationship with their director of IT, Susan Outland. Susan got me a meeting with their corporate attorney, John Banas, who had just started a few days before. John and Susan were accommodating, and after a few problems—mostly the issue described earlier as to whether they had the right to use the software for free nationwide—agreed to sign the amendment. I was extremely grateful, as there was nothing in it for them to make things easier for us. The deal with ZOLL was still on.

In addition to the audit, ZOLL completed what is known as a "due diligence" process, where they made sure we didn't have any undisclosed secrets. Lawyers peered at all our contracts, ZOLL folks talked to our customers, and Rick and Ernie asked endless questions about the inner workings of our business.

Most of the early work was done by me, David, and Bob because ZOLL didn't want to announce the deal until it was done. Because of this, they felt strongly that we shouldn't let Pinpoint staff know about the impending deal until very close to the end of the process.

In addition to audits and due diligence, we tried to get better acquainted with the WesTech business. David and I flew to Vancouver to meet with Keith Lyon, the general manager. Keith was now to report directly to me, meaning that I needed to figure out how, if at all, we wanted to change the WesTech operation. Rolf was a big advocate of "just shut it down and move it all to Boulder," but I favored a slower approach. We discovered that things were running even less smoothly than we thought, and it was hard to figure out where to start when WesTech was in Vancouver and we were in Boulder. In hindsight, perhaps Rolf's approach would have been better.

As if all that wasn't enough, there was a contract negotiation to go through. I had thought that because we had an easy time agreeing on a three-page letter of intent that the contract would be a straightforward process. Nothing could have been further from the truth. Although the letter of intent laid out the basics of the deal that wouldn't change, the ultimate contract took up two entire four-inch-thick binders. Some examples of points that had to be agreed upon included:

- They wanted a clause that said that we would give them their money back if our software had Y2K bugs. We didn't think there were any such problems but didn't want to risk everything. We finally agreed that we guaranteed "that to the best of our knowledge" there were no Y2K issues.
- We had a severance clause in our employment agreement that if ZOLL fired us for anything other than gross negligence, we were entitled to a year's pay. We wound up arguing about whether this amount would be reduced by the amount of salary we might get from a new job. We wound up splitting the difference, agreeing to reduce our severance by 50 percent of any new job's salary.
- Initially, the building that we had purchased was to be excluded from the sale, meaning that David, Bob, and I would retain ownership. However, some of the accountants were concerned that this would violate the pooling of interests rules, so we negotiated a price and included the building in the purchase.

Amazingly, and unexpectedly to us, the deal got done on the intended date: October 15, 1999. I had read different drafts of the contract so many times that my eyes were blurry. We had faxed so many contracts, invoices, and letters to the lawyers for their due diligence review that we joked that we should have just sent them the contents of our file cabinets, rather than responding piecemeal to requests for individual documents. It might have been easier.

On the day of the sale, David, Bob, and I went into the office at 6 a.m. to do some last minute faxing before our signing appointment at our lawyer's office in downtown Boulder at 8 a.m. Ernie was at ZOLL's lawyer's office in Boston, and we were to each sign the contract and then the lawyers would attach both signature pages.

Somehow we thought we would give the final contract a read at the lawyer's, but when we got there the conference table had a stack of paper several inches thick for each of us. Believe it or not, those were just the signature pages! So many different documents needed to be signed and so many copies were needed for all the people involved that it took hours to sign them all. Rob Planchard, our attorney, was there with Ginger Margolin, an attorney in his firm who had actually done all of the work. They expertly placed signature pages in front of us to sign and then whisked them away to a place where they could later figure out to which document they belonged.

All this worked reasonably well, with only a few issues raised and quickly corrected. Ernie was available all day at the other end of the phone, so we could quickly iron out any issues that required our two parties to agree on something.

Around noon, though, all hell broke loose. The ZOLL lawyers were insisting on what is called an "opinion letter" from our law firm. The letter was to say that to the best of our attorney's knowledge, Pinpoint was legitimate, the deal was good, and the company was not pledged in some other way, nor were there other shareholders who might come out of the woodwork and claim that they were entitled to a portion of the deal.

According to Rob, this opinion letter was not only hard to get, as several partners had to sign off on it, but also extremely unusual, bordering on unheard of. In addition, it would require additional work, such as examining our respective personal mortgage agreements to make sure that we hadn't used the company as collateral. Rob convinced me that the request wasn't reasonable and got me all worked up, so I pushed back and told ZOLL that the letter shouldn't be necessary. The more I tried to make my point, though, the more Ray Zemlin, ZOLL's attorney, dug his heels in. Perhaps he was concerned that our concern was an indication that we had something to hide. I was so livid that I was close to saying, "Sign today, or the deal is off. And I'm not going home to dig through my personal files." Fortunately, we were able to reach a compromise, in which our attorneys agreed to provide the opinion within a few days and their attorneys agreed to let the deal close with that promise.

It was in that context that David, Bob, and I, along with our wives, went out to celebrate that Friday night. What we thought was going to be an hour or two of routine paper signing turned into a 10-hour ordeal full of emotion. I was so angry I hardly felt like celebrating. Fortunately, the feeling wore off and we managed to have a good time.

I thought the deal was done, but that was not the case. The next morning, a Saturday, I got frantic calls from the ZOLL folks, their lawyers, and their accountants. Apparently, they had discovered a provision in our agreement that might blow the pooling of interests. Fortunately, the change they wanted was good for us. Instead of warranting something-or-other for three years, this was to be reduced to a year and a half, the maximum allowed under the pooling rules. Although this was clearly no problem for us, I didn't want to sign the change until I had tracked down our attorney.

When I finally reached him, he asked if they wanted to create an amendment, or to simply do a "slip page." Although I had never heard that term, I immediately knew what he meant. We would just change out the page that said three years for one that said 18 months. Because the signature page was at the back, this would be as simple as having someone print out the new page and inserting it into the correct document. I said to Rob, "Yes, a slip page, but it bothers me that you have a term for that."

One of the craziest things about the ZOLL deal was that it didn't cost them anything. I came to learn that publicly traded companies have a license to print money. They paid us by giving us shares. Those shares were simply issued by the company on top of all the shares that already existed. The only negative to ZOLL was that with more shares out there, the price per share might be a little less, driving the stock price down. But because Pinpoint's profits were added to ZOLL's profits, there was more value too. In the end, the deal was non-dilutive, meaning that the company was worth more on a per-share basis, even with the extra shares out there. The deal didn't cost ZOLL or their shareholders a cent.

Chapter 9 The ZOLL Years

After the long and exhausting process of selling the company there was to be no rest. ZOLL's annual sales meeting was scheduled for the week after the deal was done, with a hundred or so salespeople from around the world attending. We knew that the WesTech salespeople would be there, as would the support folks, so we tried to be as ready as we could. We wanted to immediately change the reporting structure so that the WesTech salespeople reported to Bob and not up through the ZOLL organization. That was easy to accomplish. What was harder was to have answers to all their questions. They had four salespeople and we had two. We'd decided to have a joint sales force that would sell all products, but sales territories naturally overlapped and people wanted to know what was going to happen to them. Bob and I did our best to answer their questions, but all four of the WesTech reps eventually left, one right away and the other three within a couple of years.

In addition to preparing for the sales meeting we needed to work up a budget for Ernie, which he'd requested right after the sale closed. Later I would learn about the ZOLL budgeting process and find out that a budget takes a couple of months to put together, but since it was due when the sale closed, Bob and I had to create the budget on the plane on the way to Cape Cod. It was accepted without revision. Of course, we then had to live with delivering what we had promised, which turned out to be not so easy to do.

Most important, we had to figure out what we were going to do with WesTech: not only the company, but also the product, EMS Pro. We had weekly integration meetings to plan what we were going to do, but ultimately moved everything to Boulder in stages:

- The first step was to have the sales reps report directly to Bob in Boulder.
- We decided pretty quickly that we should move support from Boston to Boulder. None of the staff wanted to relocate, so we sent Sean Kelly from our support group to Boston to become the expert.
- We decided to keep the WesTech name by calling the product WesTech EMS Pro (by Pinpoint Technologies). Eventually we dropped WesTech from the name.
- We decided to cancel WesTech's user conference that was held each fall in Vancouver and have users join our user conference in Colorado in the spring.
- We formalized their deployment process. Previously they'd contracted with customers for installation and training. We used some of the techniques we had learned through CAD and billing. We sent Ed Bodecker from our deployment department to Vancouver to become the expert.
- We froze development on the software and went into bug-fixing mode. We had discovered that none of the customers who had purchased WesTech's Windows version were actually using the software in a live

environment. The programmers were too busy implementing new features promised by sales to clean up
the code that had already been written.

- When we realized how many customers had problems
  and how big the problems really were, we froze sales of
  the product. I give a lot of credit to ZOLL for backing
  us on this decision, as WesTech operated at a big loss
  until the product was stabilized.

- Eventually, once the software was stable enough and
  customers were happy enough, we identified some key
  individuals and relocated them from Vancouver to Boulder. Of 17 programmers in Vancouver, only 3 relocated.
  We hired one or two more and that was enough to keep
  the product going.

- With development and deployment now relocated to
  Boulder, the WesTech office in Vancouver was reduced
  to Keith Lyon. Keith did some business development
  work for Pinpoint, but ultimately that didn't prove to
  be enough work to fill his time. I eventually had to fly
  up to Vancouver to let him go. Keith stayed on for a
  little while to help close down the office. Letting Keith
  go was one of the harder things I've ever had to do. It
  must also have been sad for him to see his operation
  dismantled, but the decision was just business.

In all it took about a year to get things under control, twice
as long as we had thought it would, but the problems were
twice as bad as we had thought they were, so I consider the
transition a success. The process of having the integration
meetings, uncovering the problems, and fixing them was a
lot of fun. As I was to learn later on, it's a lot more rewarding
to fix problems that others have created than to fix problems
of your own doing.

ResponseOne

In July 2000 Pinpoint purchased a small company called ResponseOne, a company that had a long history with Pinpoint.

ResponseOne was the brainchild of longtime WesTech employees Chris Berg and Marco Oballa. Back in 1998 Chris had attended Pinpoint's Summit user conference in Vail. In the Future Session at that conference, David had talked about the possibility of creating a mobile data terminal (MDT) product for the driver of the ambulance.

David and I had always felt that Chris was a lot like us and would be a tremendous asset to Pinpoint. Chris at that time was disillusioned with WesTech and wanted to leave. I talked to him at that same user conference about becoming a full-time Pinpoint employee, but we were never able to come to an agreement.

In August 1998, after the WesTech user conference at which I met Rick Packer, Bob and I spent some time with Chris and Marco discussing the possibility of Pinpoint funding a new company to create the MDT product. We were on a trip with our wives and girlfriends and had gone to Vancouver Island to go sea kayaking. We had a fun and relaxing time and between activities talked business. Again, however, we were unable to come to terms. Chris and Marco would ultimately go on to start a company without our involvement and called their product Contact!

This became a problem for Pinpoint, as we felt it was important for us to offer an MDT solution to our clients and we had no interest in just recommending Chris and Marco's product. So we began a development effort for a similar product, called Nomad.

Although we had shown Nomad to Rick and Ernie to help entice them into purchasing Pinpoint, it wasn't a very good product. Chris and Marco had done a good job of working out all the details of the product in conjunction with their beta customer, LifeCare Ambulance in Ohio.

Fortunately for us, ResponseOne began to run out of money in early 2000. Simultaneously Marco was becoming interested in other ventures and Chris wanted to move to the US to be with his then-girlfriend (and now wife), Karen Wilson. Pinpoint and ResponseOne agreed that we would purchase the company and hire Chris, who then relocated to Boulder with Karen. Contact! was renamed Nomad and Pinpoint's version of Nomad never again saw the light of day.

Chris was originally given the position of program manager in charge of the Nomad product but quickly proved to be a great asset to Pinpoint, becoming David's right-hand man and ultimately taking over the position of running the R&D department.

Pinpoint Takes a Dive

The sale to ZOLL took place in October 1999, a time when the whole world was focused on the so-called Y2K problem. Computer programs created in the '80s and early '90s had stored years in a two-digit format and were therefore unprepared for the rollover to the new millennium.

Pinpoint had begun writing its products in 1993 and had anticipated this issue, so we were able to reap some benefits from the frenzy. As customers looked to convert from their older, non-Y2K compliant systems, Pinpoint for once was able to use its youth as an advantage.

Worldwide nervousness about Y2K was pretty high, and I remember David coming up to me on the morning of December 31—my wedding day—and telling me that our Australian customer, already into the new year, had reported no problems at all. Relieved, I got married.

We did anticipate that sales would die off in the new year, but we also thought that several potential customers would wait too long, only to be let down by less up-to-date software systems. Y2K problems, of course, failed to materialize and our anticipated additional revenues from replacing failing systems never came to fruition. In January 2000 sales went to almost zero and stayed that way for four months.

In addition to Y2K, Pinpoint had other growing pains, all of which contributed to us losing money for the first time in 2000 and 2001. The factors that contributed to this downslide were:

1. Our focus on WesTech no doubt took management energy away from our core business problems. But, while this had an effect, it would be too convenient to blame our dive on being too busy fixing WesTech. Certainly, the major WesTech work had been completed by the end of 2000, so there is no blaming the poor performance in 2001 on this distraction.

2. Y2K also was a factor in our trouble in 2000. We failed to anticipate the drop-off in sales and had ramped up staffing—and therefore expenses—to a point where we were no longer profitable. As with the WesTech problem, though, Y2K's effect was present in 2000 but not 2001.

3. We didn't focus on sales and marketing. Up to 1999 Pinpoint had been a small entrepreneurial company whose sales were based on the strength of its products and services. Our sales department was no longer operating with both feet on the brakes and we were transitioning to a state of having to work harder to find new customers. This required a dedicated marketing effort that we didn't have and that required more than the two sales reps that we had covering the entire country.

To ZOLL's credit they had foreseen the sales and marketing issue prior to acquiring us. They were tremendously helpful over the next two years in providing advice and guiding us as we set up a better infrastructure and grew as a company.

Obviously they were not pleased that we were losing money, but Rick showed a lot of faith in our ability to turn things around. Only once, in the second year, did he sit me down to make sure I was focused on the problem and not an absentee president now that I had sold the company.

"If your heart's not in it anymore, Dave, we can find someone else to run the show."

"No," I said, "I'm working harder than I ever have before. I'll get this fixed."

"That's all I needed to hear," Rick said. "I'm telling the board that you're our guy to get this turned around."

In that short conversation, I certainly recognized that I was on my last leg and that if things didn't turn around soon I would be out of a job. I completely recognized this as fair and appreciated that Rick delivered the message without yelling or threatening.

Fortunately, things did in fact turn around soon after that. We hired a great sales manager, named Fred Funke, and filled out the sales roster with five full-time positions, having now replaced all the inherited WesTech reps. In addition we promoted Marcie Cary from sales coordinator to the head of an independent marketing department. Marcie spent the next two years taking marketing from nearly nothing at all to having a strong foundation, with proper advertising, trade show coordination, and direct mail. Each of these initiatives paid off and from that point to the end of my stay at Pinpoint we enjoyed eight consecutive quarters of success. In each quarter we met or often exceeded our budget, growing 58 percent and 42 percent per year over two years, all while increasing productivity and profitability and therefore contributing to ZOLL's bottom line.

Would we have been able to stay in business had we not been bought by ZOLL? I often get asked that question, and I don't know the answer. On one hand, there were a lot of new expenses related to WesTech that we wouldn't have had. On the other hand, in order to keep from running out of cash, we would have had to have layoffs. Would we have done it in time, or would we have delayed, thinking a recovery was just around the corner? It's all speculation and there is no way to know for certain.

Chapter 10 Why End It?

It was certainly Rolf and Rick's biggest concern.

"Before we buy you," they said, "we want to be sure that you're going to stick around."

"Of course I'm going to stick around," I said. "I'm too young to retire and I love Pinpoint too much."

That's what I said and I meant it. And for the first year or so it remained true. I enjoyed working on fixing WesTech. I enjoyed learning about the ins and outs of working for a publicly traded company.

However, it gradually became drudgery. You had to keep selling more, you were only as good as your most recent quarter, you had to watch to make sure customers didn't owe you too much, and you had to deal with audits, accountants, revenue recognition policies, and countless other details. Pinpoint was no longer the company it had been in the early days. Products and customers were a means to an end rather than the purpose itself. I felt like I had become a corporate drone; I yearned for the early days when it was just a few of us trying to make something out of nothing.

It only took one year for me to realize that I wasn't going to be in it for the long haul. At the second sales meeting that Bob and I attended, a year into the acquisition, I noticed that ZOLL sales reps had tenure ribbons on their name badges that said "five years" or "10 years."

"I should have one that says three left," I said to Bob.

Although nothing in my employment agreement or the acquisition agreement compelled me to stay, I felt that I owed ZOLL four years. Rick and I had never discussed an exact four-year time frame, but we did have a four-year employment agreement and we had promised not to sell a portion of stock for four years. When I promised Rick that I was staying, it felt like a four-year promise.

After that sales meeting, I warned Rick about how I felt. He took it well and said that his hope was that after Pinpoint turned around and started making money again, I would enjoy it more.

"That's possible," I said, "but I doubt it."

A year later I had the same conversation with him and let him know that things were better at Pinpoint, but that I still wanted to leave in two years.

"Okay," he said. "Just give me plenty of notice." A year later, I gave a year's notice.

The New Guy

I spent my final year at Pinpoint trying to get the company in the best possible shape for a new president. I took care of some things that I thought the new president might not want to be burdened with, such as hiring a comptroller to oversee the accounting details.

Rick oversaw the selection of my replacement. No internal candidates, either at ZOLL or Pinpoint, seemed appropriate. Neither David nor Bob was interested in applying, so Rick created a detailed job description and a set of requirements with help and involvement from the three of us.

He assigned ZOLL's internal recruiter, John Bogosian, the job of finding suitable candidates. Rick flew out to Colorado, where he, John, and I met with a half dozen or so candidates John had identified as being at the top of the pile.

After those interviews, I did first interviews with ten or so more individuals. From those interviews and the ones in the first group, we sent four candidates to ZOLL to meet with the top executives there. From this exercise the list was narrowed to two, who then met with some key people at Pinpoint. In the end Vane Clayton was selected.

Vane started in September 2003 and took control at the beginning of the new fiscal year in October. I stayed around to help out and answer questions until my last day, October 31, 2003.

When I left the Pinpoint building on that Friday afternoon, it was a sad day. I had spent most of the day saying goodbye to people I had worked with, some for as long as 10 years. I had emptied out my desk and found old pictures of David and me at the Indianapolis 500 in 1995, Bob and me doing the AID deployment in the same year, and many other memories.

A few days earlier, Rick had asked me what the strangest thing was about leaving. "I've probably had lunch with David Cohen five out of seven days for the past 13 years," I said.

Looking Back

So how did a bunch of young hooligans manage to build a profitable, $13 million company with virtually no investment? Luck certainly played a big part, but here are some of the things I think we did right:

- *We were in the right place at the right time and had the vision to recognize it.* In 1994 we recognized that a Windows-based dispatch system had a place in the ambulance marketplace. While competitors were still focused on old technology, we were able to get ahead.
- *We stayed focused.* We knew our strength, which was providing software to ambulance companies. Along the way there were countless temptations to go off in a different direction. Early on we almost took a contract to adapt our system for courier companies. People tried to convince us that our dispatch system would work for locksmiths and mobile diagnostic devices. We worked very hard to stay out of the business of reselling hardware. All of these decisions allowed us to not waste our effort learning new things.
- *We provided a great work environment.* Our employees liked coming to work and contributing. The energy put into creating an enjoyable environment was worth it for us, even though it's something frequently ignored by companies.
- *We cared about providing great products and great services.* This was one of our core beliefs and we lived it every day. If you start to analyze whether a particular feature is good for profits or if an expense is really necessary, quality suffers and it hurts you in the long run. Even though we had a 95 percent satisfaction rate from our customers, we wanted it to be higher.

What I Learned about Vision, Strategy, and Execution

In the introduction I mentioned that I learned that words matter and that they matter a lot. I changed the subtitle because I now believe, after some reflection and experience as CEO of Techstars, that vision, along with strategy and execution, are fundamental ingredients to successfully building a sustainable business. I think of vision as the destination, strategy as the path to get there, and execution as the steps and rocks along the way.

At Pinpoint we didn't articulate a vision, but we always had the belief that we had a destination. We saw a need for software in the niche we were operating in, and we realized that Microsoft Windows could be capitalized to change how ambulance companies dispatched vehicles. And we learned that the world hadn't recognized that yet. We saw enough of the future to realize we could get there first.

Today, I would say that we were opportunistic, that we saw a way to build a better mousetrap and displace the incumbents. But that is the reality for most startups: you create a better technology and get to the future before your competitors. It's only after the mad scramble to get to consistent revenues that you realize how vision, strategy, and execution played out as the foundation to a sustainable business.

What's Next?

In 2004, when I finished the first edition of this book, I faced the prospect of what I was going to do next. I was 39 years old, and although I had two small children, I didn't think I could stay at home for a long period of time. My brain was going to call me back to action soon.

For my whole career I had drifted from one opportunity to another, guided by luck and by my instincts more than by any grand plan.

As I considered my options—teaching, going back to school for a degree in a completely different discipline, helping startup companies learn from our experiences, or starting up a new business—I realized that I had never in my life been on a job interview.

Chapter 11 After Pinpoint

I always knew I wouldn't be able to sit still for long. I scoffed at people who said that I had retired at the age of 39. If I were to stay home, my wife said that the only one who would be more frustrated than me would be her. I decided that I wasn't going to do another startup, concluding that I'd been there and done that, but I didn't know what I was going to do. My retirement lasted eight months, during which time I wrote this book.

iContact

David and Bob decided that they were going to leave Pinpoint soon after I did. They wanted to do another startup but hadn't settled on an idea. For a while I was deluded with the notion that I wouldn't join them, but eventually I realized that I couldn't resist. Once I told them I was in, we sat down for an afternoon brainstorming session at a Chili's restaurant in Boulder. David and Bob had a list of seven ideas, each one different from the next. I don't remember what they were, but the one we picked was the idea of using your cell phone to identify which friends were nearby so as to be able to connect with them.

This was in 2004, in the era before Facebook and iPhones, when social networking wasn't mainstream and cell phones weren't open for applications. Our experience was in selling enterprise software to businesses, so this was about as different as different could be. But that was the point: we wanted to prove that we had the ability to do something different. Plus, we wanted to create something that would be a household name and we felt that would be easier to do in a B2C (business-to-consumer) environment.

Within days we had picked a company name (iCentric), secured the domain name, incorporated, picked a product name (iContact), and found an office.

We funded it ourselves, still inexperienced in the fundraising process and skeptical after our experiences at Pinpoint. But a funny thing happened: a lot of people came out of the woodwork saying, "I want in." Friends, family, Pinpoint employees, and even Pinpoint customers wanted to have a stake. Now that we'd built a successful company and had a nice exit, everyone assumed we would succeed.

We didn't really need the money, but we thought that it would be neat for these investors to have a stake in our success and would help us get the product off the ground, so we raised what I now know is called an "FFF round" (friends, family, and fools).

We hired a programmer named Dave Taubler and set to work on creating a product. The biggest problem was getting the application installed on cell phones. In 2004 cell phone carriers had "decks," a series of applications that came preinstalled on phones. There wasn't an app store ecosystem for startups that created their own applications. We tried to lobby carriers to include us, to no avail.

So we pivoted and focused on the back end, creating a web-based social network. At the time Friendster had just failed but Myspace was doing well. We kept hearing about a company called Facebook, but their product was only available to students with an .edu email address so we didn't worry about them too much.

We made a go of it but never did get traction. The novel idea was the mobile capability, as neither Myspace nor Facebook had this, but until the iPhone was launched in 2007 there was no way for mobile app developers to get their products distributed. The pivot gave us something to do, but it didn't set us apart. We survived for a while but then decided to shut down. iContact turned out to be an idea ahead of its time.

One of the things we were the most proud of was that we recognized early on that iContact wasn't going to be a success. We still had plenty of cash, but rather than keeping things going we decided to return it to our investors—they were our friends and family, after all. Our personal investment was lost, but we returned 78 percent to our investors.

Angel Investing

Again faced with the prospect of what to do next, David and I decided to explore the world of angel investing. We attended a few pitch sessions organized by various groups in Colorado and eventually stumbled onto a group called CTEK, which was run by Gary Held and was where we met Nicole Glaros, later to become a longtime managing director and partner at Techstars.

The process was new to us: a group of investors paid $1,000 a year each for the right to hear pitches. The companies would pay to pitch and the investors would be expected to make at least one investment per year in order to continue to participate in the group.

Although we made a few investments and met some great people and companies, we found the process to be frustrating. The companies had the same problems we had always had and no way to get good advice, plus the investing process seemed to be set up more for the investors than the entrepreneurs. David and I used to brainstorm about how it could be done better on our drive back home from CTEK in Denver.

The Idea for Techstars

The idea for Techstars came out of David's head fully formed and arrived via email.

From: David Cohen
Sent: Wednesday, February 08, 2006, 10:12 a.m.
To: David Brown

I'm just thinking this can be one of the Boomtown businesses.[1] Providing seed capital to startups with only an idea.
The concept:

1. We take applications on the website. Only seed-stage companies need apply (those with passionate people and an idea, but with no way to get going or who are not sure they can do it on their own—maybe just need a kick in the ass and someone to believe in them).

2. We fly or drive to interview the ones that sound good (perhaps organizing small tours) or have them come here on our dime.

3. We offer the promising ones $10K for a 2 percent noncontrolling interest—and no board seat—in their company. They have to come to Boulder for two to three months to start the company up.

---

[1] "Boomtown" was our code name for our next company, based on a hit song called "Welcome to the Boomtown" by, wait for it, David and David.

a. They can work in our offices or in a hotel or wherever they want. We provide Internet connections, a little office space, etc.

b. They can use the $10K however they want.

c. We have the option to buy an additional 2 percent interest in the company for another $10K at the end of the two- to three-month period.

d. We provide free consulting while they're here, including product feedback, how-to advice, etc.

e. We organize weekly (or biweekly) dinners with CTEK, IP lawyers, tech experts, etc. (basically using our contacts to get people to donate a little time).

4. Based on how they do while they're here, we decide if we want to invest more when they leave. This should be easy, since you're really evaluating the people as much as the product (do they work all kinds of hours? do they have passion?).

5. If they want, they can stay in Boulder and grow their company here, working in our office space (renting it). Perhaps we have some kind of "space+connectivity+consulting" lease rate.

The only drawback I can think of is that we'd probably need to get a slightly nicer office to really attract companies. We'd have to look successful and have an environment with couches, whiteboards, etc. if they decide to work there. But we could grow that over time once we get a few companies and have a good feeling that the concept is working.

I am thinking I'll start working on the website. Are you cool with putting this kind of info/offer up on the boomtown site? We don't have to actually do it, I suppose, but we can at least start taking applications and see what's what. Maybe generate a little word of mouth somehow, and who knows. We can start with a summer program this year. Sublet or rent some open office space from this place for just three months or something. Start trying to spread the word a little bit on college campuses, especially CU, CSU, DU, etc.

Thoughts? I think it sounds really cool. Yeah, we have no idea what we're doing. I feel like angel groups are really a different level of money. That's for companies who need $100K or $500K. I want to get them before they know they need that, so we can get an early interest and hook them up with CTEK or whoever (or even us) when they need more money later on.

* * *

From: David Brown
Sent: Wednesday, February 08, 2006, 10:47 a.m.
To: David Cohen

Yes, something like that is what I meant by being our own angel group (I really should call it mini-angel group, because it would be designed for much smaller—and riskier—companies). There are a lot of good ideas in your email. We should talk them out some more.

One thought is that I think we should try to focus on Boulder people first. Somehow I feel like there are a lot of young up-and-coming entrepreneurs locally. We can always expand if that doesn't yield any applications.

* * *

From: David Cohen
Sent: Wednesday, February 08, 2006, 10:51 a.m.
To: David Brown

Maybe we can get a private lunch today? I think it's so cool. My only concerns would be credibility (do we have enough?) and legal advice.

* * *

From: David Brown
Sent: Wednesday, February 08, 2006, 11:09 a.m.
To: David Cohen

I really think there have to be some supersmart CU students willing to work 80 hours a week on a great idea they have.

* * *

From: David Cohen
Sent: Wednesday, February 08, 2006, 11:15 a.m.
To: David Brown

For sure. The question is how do you find them?

* * *

From: David Brown
Date: Wednesday, February 8, 2006, 11:16:50 a.m.
To: David Cohen

Maybe we should contact the business school?

What's amazing to me about this email is how true to the eventual model it was. The equity strategy, mentorship, and communal environment are all the underpinnings of Techstars to this day.

Concept to Reality

We knew that in order to get the idea off the ground we would need a bigger megaphone than we were able to provide. Although we had been successful entrepreneurs, David and I lacked any personal brand awareness. David decided to pitch the idea to Brad Feld, one of Colorado's best-known and respected venture captialists. Brad had a practice at the time of having what he called "random days," which were days set aside to meet with anyone who piqued his interest. David reached out to Brad and was a little surprised when Brad's assistant came back with "Brad would like to meet with you a month from next Tuesday for 15 minutes."

The meeting went well because Brad committed on the spot. Agreeing that we needed a megaphone, he asked if he could bring in his friend, prominent Colorado investor and entrepreneur Jared Polis (now Colorado's governor). Brad's story is that when he called Jared and said, "I have a great opportunity—can I tell you about it?," Jared responded with "I'm in! What is it?," in that order. Jared's story is that when Brad tells you that he has a great opportunity, you'd be a fool to say anything else.

With that, Techstars was off to the races. A simple website, an office that we called "the bunker" in the basement of a building, and a few months later, the Boulder class of 2007 was inaugurated. With David as managing director, it would go on to be one of many successful classes in Techstars' history.

Conclusion

*N*o *Vision All Drive* is a personal narrative, a chronicle, of the events, people, companies, and markets I was involved with during the early stage of my entrepreneurial career. When I first sat down to write my story, I thought that my journey was singularly unique, because I started my career in a government job in Montreal and eventually ended up in Boulder, Colorado. Now, after spending years running Techstars and working with thousands of entrepreneurs, I realize that my story is very similar to other entrepreneurs.

In the early days, I never thought of myself as an entrepreneur and had no knowledge of business before I started down that path. I didn't have any exposure to business as a child and I didn't take any business classes in college. I only became involved in entrepreneurship by chance, when Martin Nathanson, my first manager in the government job, told me that he was starting his own business and I became employee no. 1.

Frankly, that's true of a lot of the founders we see at Techstars. They have zero experience in building a business, in taking an idea and building a business around that, and they're unfamiliar about all the little steps that need to take place to be successful, to create a sustainable business. I learned more about failure from Martin than anything else because he was enamored with the technology and couldn't come up with a business model. But I've also seen that same characteristic countless times with founders we work with at Techstars.

Many founders believe that if they can get the "best" technology out in the market they'll be successful, only to find out that markets rarely reward the "best" product. Or founders with deep technical expertise hire a businessperson to "run the company," sometimes with dismal results.

While Martin had an idea and a cool technology, David Cohen had a passion to start a business, and together we decided to take the technology we created at ADS to the market. (Later, David, Bob Durkin, and I sat at a Chili's restaurant in Boulder, created a list of seven ideas, and picked one to form a business around.) I have found that there are people passionate about an idea and they build a business around that, and people passionate about building a business and they find an idea to bring to their business. Both approaches work for entrepreneurs.

There are other themes and lessons within the book that strike me as important. Perhaps the most important lesson is that we deeply understood our customer, the problems they faced, and the solution our software provided. We didn't run customer focus groups or look at demographic trends, and if "big data" had been around then, we wouldn't have used it. But we *knew* our customers. We went to their location, worked with their employees, spent time with them, shared meals with them, and learned about their personal lives. We created our Summit User Conference to provide a forum for learning and sharing, not as a way to sell them something.

It wasn't easy. Looking back on it, it was a grind, but we did whatever it took for our customers. We moved around the country, lived with each other, traveled by ambulance to the job site, worked long hours weeks and months at a time, and took huge personal and financial risks. We were rewarded with the ability to create a sustainable business. In hindsight, there's nothing more gratifying than starting a business, providing a real solution to customers who will gladly pay you, and creating jobs and opportunities for others. At Techstars, we continue our relentless customer focus, create jobs and opportunities for our employees, and find it immensely gratifying to operate a sustainable and growing business.

Another thing that struck me about my Pinpoint experience was our focus on experiments and learning, not just on generating more sales. Many people may consider our sale to Queensland Ambulance Service to be a failure since we only got one sale, but we saw it as a success because we learned important things. We learned the process of international sales, the specifications for date and phone formats, translating US measurements to metric units, and we learned how to provide support and service long distance. At Sweet Computer Services we learned to avoid litigation and that it's better to give up something to close the chapter and move on. We learned that while distributorships have the advantage of a sales staff and those people know the local laws, taxes, and customers, the great disadvantage is that you give up control over your product and sales process using distributors. Finally, we negotiated with Constellation Software to be acquired in good faith, but we approached it as a learning opportunity. We were completely unfamiliar with selling a company, and we wanted to understand how the acquisition process worked.

One important decision-making rule we created in the very beginning, and not related to Pinpoint—initially—was the idea that any of us could veto an idea. We started doing this socially, in choosing where to eat for lunch. If one of us didn't like what the other suggested, we'd just veto it. We eventually used this approach for more significant decisions. When we decided to relocate from Florida, Arizona, and New York so that we could all work together in one place, we each listed several locations that were exciting for us. But we each also had a "veto" to cross off a location that we really didn't want to go to. Boulder was the only remaining location after that process. The veto rule is something we used in the early days of Techstars, although we removed it as we grew.

Reflecting back on my experience at Pinpoint I understand now that a lot of our success stemmed from the ethos that we created. We were transparent and honest with John Shermyen about our desire to start a company that could compete with ADS. That transparency and honesty also applied to how we treated each other. We didn't have titles or big egos on what role we played, we communicated regularly, shared our innermost thoughts, and we had fun together. We ran our office like it was our living room, wearing t-shirts and shorts, having flexible schedules, providing food, drinks, and snacks that we could all share. We realized that it's impossible to compartmentalize work life and personal life, and we made very little distinction between the two. We were all friends. In a startup it's important that the founders be friends, that they like and trust each other. As a company grows it's important for the leadership team, or any "team" to be friends, so that ideas and problems can be shared and taken seriously.

The ethos that we created at Pinpoint is embodied in the core beliefs that David Cohen wrote out, but those core beliefs emerged long after we started working together. They were more of an affirmation of what we had been doing than an aspiration of what we would be doing. And those core beliefs are part of the DNA at Techstars, and in large measure have contributed to the growth and success of the company.

In retrospect, we created and operated Pinpoint not based on a blueprint, book, or advice from experts, but based on our belief in how we wanted to treat people and be treated by others: transparency, honesty, trust, learning, and fun. We also spent most of our time in execution mode—creating and refining our dispatching software, implementing it in different companies, and refining it. We didn't start with a vision, core values, and core beliefs. Now that I have several decades' experience starting and running businesses, and countless interactions with startup founders, I believe that spending some time articulating core values, core beliefs, a vision statement, or any other document that provides guiding principles early in a startup's life is time well spent. In fact, efforts to create guiding principles are often the only thing worth doing early on to solve a problem that does not yet exist. Everything else is like figuring out where you are going to park the company jet. Just wait until you have a jet.

When I created the title, *No Vision All Drive*, it was meant to refer to David, Bob, and myself who, as young entrepreneurs, weren't focused on vision. Now, 30 years later, we have learned the importance of focusing on vision early, but we have also learned that in the early stages of building a company, founders would do well to focus on the more fine-grained and tangible parts of their business. How do we want to treat each other? How do we show respect to others? Where do we draw a line in the sand? What will we not do? Vision and strategy are important, but execution is where the rubber meets the road. At Pinpoint we started executing right away, and we continued executing until we sold the company. It's the daily grind where the day-to-day work happens, and that makes the vision a reality.

Pinpoint was not a household name, it did not generate interest from investors or venture capitalists, and we never grew to be a billion-dollar business, although it's still profitable a quarter century after our founding. But everything I learned at Pinpoint has had a direct bearing on Techstars, and Techstars far exceeds Pinpoint on every metric.

One final thought about my entrepreneurial career emerged after Pinpoint was sold and iContact failed. I learned the importance of humility. That's something that every

Epilogue

I could have stayed on with David at Techstars, but I decided to return to ZOLL, where the company was in a little trouble and in need of a turnaround. When David asked me why I wanted to return to a big company, I said that you could do so much more with 100 people (my team's size at the time) versus just 2 and David responded, "Yeah, about twice as much." So true.

I stayed at ZOLL for seven more years, and under David's leadership Techstars grew rapidly during that time, expanding into multiple cities and creating a brand synonymous with helping entrepreneurs. He also raised two venture funds to help invest in the best entrepreneurs and brought on partners Molly Nasky and Mark Solon.

ZOLL had tripled in size since my return and was doing very well. I was enjoying my time at the company and expected to spend the rest of my career there. David and I had a long-standing arrangement to play racquetball every Friday morning unless one of us was traveling (it turns out we played only about once a quarter). In early 2013 after one of those games, David asked if I would return to Techstars as a partner. We talked about how we'd worked together our whole careers and how well we complemented each other's skill sets.

I couldn't say no.

Since 2013, I have been running Techstars, the idea first conceived in David's email. Since that inauspicious start, Techstars has wildly exceeded my expectations. Techstars is a global leader in entrepreneurship and innovation working with entrepreneurs, mentors, community leaders, investors, global corporations, governments, and universities. From that first accelerator in Boulder in 2007 we now have 48 accelerators in 43 countries, have nearly 1,500 graduates and over 10,000 mentors involved in the accelerators, offer more than 1,000 startup weekends each year, and have a truly global community of contributors. Yet many of the principles we started at Pinpoint—a focus on customers, a "work hard, play hard" culture, an openness to exploring ideas, a commitment to moving fast, and having a lot of fun along the way—are core principles of Techstars.

I couldn't possibly have projected this career when I left Montreal for Florida decades ago, but the risks and hard work have been worth it.

About the Author

Originally from Montreal, Canada, **David Brown** is a serial entrepreneur. David has founded three software startups and has been involved with two others. David is one of the original founders of Pinpoint Technologies, now part of ZOLL Medical Corporation. He served as president of the company from its founding to its position as an industry leader with over $50 million per year in revenue and over 250 employees. David later cofounded Techstars in 2006 with David Cohen, Brad Feld, and Jared Polis. David is CEO of Techstars, the worldwide network that helps entrepreneurs succeed. In a little over a dozen years since its founding, Techstars' accelerators have funded more than 1,700 companies in more than 30 locations in 13 countries. Nearly 90 percent of the startups are successful: they have become profitable, have been bought by companies such as Google, Salesforce, Microsoft, and Facebook, and they have gone on to raise more than $7 billion in capital. David lives in Boulder, Colorado, with his wife, Kris, and their two children.

Index